Any Damn Thing

A True Tale of Duty and Defiance

Janice Kenyon

First Impression – 2003

ISBN 1 84323 206 5

This book is published with the financial support of the
Welsh Books Council.

Printed in Wales by
Gomer Press, Llandysul, Ceredigion

CONTENTS

FOREWORD

When the scribble *A.D.T.* appeared on a prescription pad in a Welsh General Practitioner's dispensary, a miner was given *Any Damn Thing* – usually a small bottle of Rose Water. *A.D.T.* was a private and sympathetic signal between dispenser daughter and doctor father, allowing the patient to claim a day of relief from going down. Their clandestine operation originated in the 1920s, before the demise of the Welsh coal-mining industry and remained a secret, untold and unknown by anyone until it was exposed in the 1980s. And with the exposure of this one secret, a whole series of revelations was brought to light, telling the truly remarkable tale of a seemingly ordinary woman.

The turning point was the death in 1976 of a Scottish doctor, Bill Henry, who had practised in Moorends, Yorkshire for almost thirty years. Only then did his Welsh wife, Marjorie Thomas Henry, begin speaking about her life abroad before the Great War; her adventures during that war; and her years at Hirwaun, the town of her birth high in the Cynon Valley in mid Glamorgan, South Wales. Her stories were amazing, amusing, even shocking to her family.

Her life as a conventional, conservative, courageous wife and mother in a Yorkshire mining town from 1926 to 1955 was all her family and friends had known. Retirement near the sea in Sussex brought a quiet contentment, occasionally jarred by suppressed memories or postcard correspondence with pre-First World War school friends in Germany. By the time of her husband's death in 1976, almost all of Marjorie's Welsh family from the early part of the century had died, except for her younger sister Dorothy who lived until 1984, and Dorothy's son who remembered his favourite aunt from when he was six years old and lived with her in Wales. But with the demise of the Welsh doctor's family came a corresponding decline in the intrepid eldest daughter's restraint.

Finally, with the death of Bill, she could tell her story. But only with much prompting. It took an outsider – the author of this book – to coax from the reluctant heroine the anecdotes and eventually the written memoirs that form the basis of *Any Damn Thing*. Interviews with frail Marjorie, who lived the last decade of her ninety-seven years in a nursing home, disclosed remarkable souvenirs of unsung escapades in foreign lands. First she unveiled the series of portrait photos, circa 1914, that were taken for a long ago fiancé in France. Then there were photographs of swimmers in Edwardian costumes taken by the French seashore, with Marjorie amongst them. She also appeared in her fashionable 1912 picture hat or turban-style cloche, with the Brittany coast as background. There was even one of her in traditional Breton costume. Her scattered early twentieth century album also showcased a well-dressed French family in group photographs where a dapper young man in a bowler hat was a distinct and recurring presence. There were images of war casualties and nurses in First World War uniforms. Marjorie pointed to herself several times – and ultimately a handsome French pilot: Louis, that dapper young man in the bowler hat, who was also the lost fiancé.

At last, this extraordinary tale of daring defiance, brief but brutal in its intensity, was told. The attempt to break from family tradition, the interference of the Great War, the denial of dreams – all have been told before; but Marjorie's telling is especially poignant. She unravels history as she describes a working, professional-class daughter from Wales cast onto the European stage. In love with a foreigner, she is torn by a filial duty that was dangerously close to martyrdom, before being saved in her final hour of youth by a professional man from Scotland.

No one had heard these stories before these unveilings. Unfortunately, they surfaced when Marjorie was already in her precarious waning years. She lived almost a century, alert for most of that time, but in the latter years unable to write or see or hear easily. Hence, her story is part broken anecdote; part coherent written memoirs; and part taped interviews where she responded to specific questions. There is much that is missing, but after sixty-five years her box of memorabilia lay open, with its drawings of Zouave camels, and its photographs of butterfly nets and a World War One pilot, telling us in their turn *Any Damn Thing*.

Acknowledgements

Marjorie's story would not have been written without the generosity and contributions of both time and information from many sources. Facts were researched, the historical significance of the story emerged, and encouragement flowed. Dr. Ross Henry, Marjorie's son and my husband, is the mainstay of this book, both because of his unstinting support and also his help with research and translations. Together we traced his mother's footsteps across Germany and France and to the Cynon Valley in South Wales, Marjorie's lilting Welsh accent whispering in our ears, encouraging us to tell her story, wishing us good luck. It is our hope that her wish has come true. To both Ross and his mum, I am thankful for letting me tell their story.

Thanks to everyone in the Thomas and Henry families. Their unflagging interest along with assistance in researching family records and photos have been invaluable.

I am also grateful to Howell's School at Llandaff, Wales and especially Jean Ballinger for information on the school in the early twentieth century; Thomas Cook Archives at Peterborough, U.K. and Paul Smith, company Archivist, for travel schedules and information 1909 to 1925; Heinrich Heine University, Düsseldorf, Germany and Professor Dr. Gisela Miller-Kipp and her assistant Ms. Hildegard Jakobs for information on early finishing schools in Düsseldorf; Stadtmuseum, Weimar, Germany and historian Christa Graeve for information on early finishing schools in Weimar plus articles on the Dürckheim family; University of Rennes, Rennes, France Bibliothèque and Marie-Francoise Hubert for assistance in locating the Gérard-Varet family; the Cynon Valley Museum in Aberdare, Wales and Gareth Gill, historian and Belinda Bajai, receptionist; the people of Hirwaun and their kind remembrances of the Thomas family;

9

Geneviève and David Gérard-Varet of Marseille, France for their permission to reproduce photos concerning their family.

Francesca Rhydderch, former editor at Gomer Press did not waver in her determination to bring *Any Damn Thing* into print; Ceri Wyn Jones, editor Gomer Press, has taken on the job of bringing everything together, and The Arts Council of Wales has given financial support. To Gomer Press and all of these contributors – a humble thank you!

Janice Kenyon,
Canmore,
Alberta,
Canada.

Chapter 1

ORIGINS: 1891 TO 1909 IN WALES

Rose Cottage, Hirwaun, Glamorgan, South Wales. October 27, 1891. Margaret Gwendolyn eases into the lives of Sarah Jane (Jeanie) and Ieuan Thomas. She is their first-born, the ease of her birth a contradiction to her feisty temperament. It isn't until a few years later that her exuberance is quelled, at least for those years when her childhood could be controlled by her strict mother. But there is a legacy, a birthright of inquisitiveness and conviviality that surfaces after her childhood, almost like a ghost. Perhaps a Welsh ghost, a kind of *Gwenhwyfar* inherited from the bard Myfyr Emlyn, her grandfather.

Rose Cottage is a small terrace house, sandwiched between the homes of the local shop owner and station master. Ieuan Thomas of Rose Cottage is the General Practitioner for the area. After qualifying with M.B. and Ch.B. degrees from Edinburgh University in 1888, his first job at Hirwaun quickly leads to his assuming the practice when the senior doctor dies. Here he remains for forty-five years, the only G.P. for a population of three to four thousand.

Back in the beginning, the doctor's growing family outgrows Rose Cottage, and by the time Dorothy is born seventeen months after Margaret, the family has moved to Tyclyd, meaning 'cosy house'. It is a large house, a good place in which to bring up children as it has two different storeys, one at street level and one at garden level; and long dark passages and various living spaces. At the end of 1898 Tyclyd houses five children – two girls followed by three boys; a governess; the family dog; at least two live-in maids; and many years later Margaret recalls:

> There was a big kitchen with flagged floors sanded over once a week and scrubbed. When Father expected a dose of

vaccinations for babies, he would notify about a dozen mothers and babies, especially if they lived on farms in outlying districts. When the kitchen was full of babies ready to be vaccinated, Father would break a tube of vaccine, puncture the baby's arm, and blow some vaccine onto the puncture site and on to another site, too.

By the turn of the century Ieuan has become active in the local shooting club whilst Jeanie insists on raising her own chickens. Britain has celebrated the Diamond Jubilee of Queen Victoria, and the high-grade coal fields of South Wales are supplying the steam-driven machines of a newly industrialized world. Hirwaun is a bustling railroad junction high on the Cynon on the northern border of mid Glamorgan; it is one valley east of the Rhondda and a vale west of the Taff. The Brecon Beacons beckon to the north; at almost 700 feet above sea level Hirwaun Common looms as a foothill plateau.

Margaret Thomas, now known as Marjorie, enjoys her *tomboy* freedom in spite of her mother. Every eighteen months or so her father takes her by train and coach to stay with Jeanie's parents in Haverfordwest in Pembrokeshire. Jeanie's father, Michael White, is from Ireland, and works as a solicitor's cashier, whilst her mother, Granny Emily, is a daughter of the renowned Llewellin churn makers. Since the 1820s, the Llewellin Churn Factory on the banks of the River Cleddau has designed, patented, and manufactured products that have won prizes and revolutionized the production of butter around the world. Trade is brisk for the churns made from imported teak and until 1853 and the coming of the railway, they are shipped direct from the port at Haverfordwest.

When Marjorie is a young child, her regular visits to Granny and Grandad White are welcome interludes. Here she can run 'round and round the mulberry bush' with her cousins amongst the churns piled by the river-front factory, or chase hoops up the hill to Dark Street where Granny and Grandad White live. But after a few weeks, her freedom is subdued by Ieuan's reappearance. When they arrive back home, there is a new sibling to greet them.

The Reverend Benjamin Thomas, Ieuan's father, is a different intrigue. No churns, no manufacturing. He and his second wife, who is nameless in Marjorie's family history notes in spite of being the mother of Benjamin's five children, live in Narberth, approximately ten miles east of Haverfordwest. A prominent Baptist minister, lecturer, and eisteddfod conductor, he is also well known as a poet, writing under his bardic name of Myfyr Emlyn. Indeed, he is afforded Druidic status in the Gorsedd of Bards, for a literary career that includes several biographies as well as publications of his poems in both Welsh and English, one version being edited by William Morris in 1898. After the death of his first wife Margaret George, who is remembered as the subject of one of his poems and who died childless, he marries at the age of forty-two the widow of David Lewis. Four of their five children live to adulthood.

Ieuan, the eldest, becomes a doctor and marries a local Welsh woman; Willie pursues a career as a chemist, marries an American and works in southern France; Bessie marries a Welsh business man and lives in England; Margaret moves to America with her American husband. By the end of the nineteenth century most of Benjamin Thomas's family have scattered, their professional training and mixed marriages separating them from their Welsh roots as well as their native language. The only child to remain and to raise his family in Wales is Ieuan, but he later would quote only a phrase or folk song to his children in Welsh as he was probably forbidden any more than that by a social-climbing Welsh wife who saw speaking English as the proper way up the ladder. English was also the language for future security; many native Welshmen believed that English speakers had the better chance for success in their chosen business or professional careers.

Grandfather Benjamin died when Marjorie was two years old, his death followed in a few months by that of his wife, neither leaving behind any lasting religious legacy for their children or their grandchildren. Jeanie, no doubt, saw Nonconformist Chapel attendance as a plebeian gesture, a mark of lower class that could be eradicated by attendance at the proper English-speaking Welsh Anglican Church. Discipline at home was severe, especially from Jeanie, but repentance before God was not a driving force behind her acerbity. The reasons given were based on expectations of how ladies of their class should behave.

Marjorie recalled:

> As a child, I never walked sedately but was always jigging about and whistling and singing the topical ditties of the time: so when I was about five or six, Mother took me and said "Little ladies don't behave like that. You must stop this whistling and singing at the top of your voice from now on." And so I was squashed and squashed forever, and never let go again.

Marjorie never became proficient in her native language in spite of becoming fluent in both German and French. Welsh was not spoken at her school or amongst the professional class that was her mother's consuming aspiration. Spanning the end of the Victorian age through Edwardian times and carrying into the Georgian period, Jeanie was a virtuous example of the rigid class hierarchy of her time. Social customs as well as domestic policies for the doctor's family amongst the coal miners were ruled by Jeanie's credence of proper middle-professional class behaviour. She did not waver in her attitudes or relax her discipline, and remained implacable in her demands on her children, especially Marjorie, the eldest.

Marjorie related several anecdotes regarding early harsh dealings from her mother. Being locked in a cupboard for misbehaving was a popular hangover from Victorian days and one which she did not escape. There was a storage room under the stairs where she remembers spending 'an awful night'. For the rest of her life, Marjorie was not comfortable with confining spaces; even the 'dreadful Alps, those high crushing mountains' were oppressive.

Marjorie wrote:

> Father was the one with the most mother-feeling in his being because I remember being very frightened of thunderstorms which were very bad at Hirwaun, and I would creep along to my parents' bedroom and beg to be taken into bed. Only once was I

14

taken in and cuddled by my father. Otherwise Mother would take me down a long dark passage, open a door into another long dark corridor into a back stair which led to the street. They had heavy doors which were closed at night. I would creep along in the dark to the end of the passage to the maids' large bedroom – there were nearly always two in the house – and they would let me sleep between them in their large feather bed until the storm was over. Then they would take me to my bedroom and my sister Dorothy who was of no use to me as a companion.

There seemed to be more than sibling rivalry between the two daughters of the family. Marjorie, the *tomboy*, whose early musical talents had been squashed, had learnt at a young age not to cry, and could protect herself. Dorothy, seventeen months younger, cried easily, especially when she wanted something, and did not accept her older sister's protective shield. While a streak of independence ran in both sisters, their personalities were so different that one wonders if they came from the same family. Even their adult recollections of their early childhood were contradictory, and not without enmity.

Their early education followed parallel paths. They at first went together, when Marjorie was about ten, to a boarding school at Porthcawl on the coast: two privileged waifs from the coal district undertaking the thirty-five mile journey by train probably only between terms. Run by three German women, the school was Marjorie's first taste of a foreign education. She said, 'I don't think we learned much but we were quite happy.'

Before Porthcawl, the girls were taught at home by a governess, 'usually staid and elderly', and on whom they were always playing tricks. There was a nursemaid named Ellen of whom they were very fond and who was followed by Douglas whom they disliked very much. When they stole her keys from her chatelaine, or rubbed out the painstaking sums to be copied from her chalkboard, sparks flew and there was 'a lot of trouble'. Neither sister can claim exemption from these escapades. Perhaps they taught Marjorie some survival tactics. Dorothy wasn't interested.

After three years at Porthcawl, the girls were sent to Howell's School at Llandaff near Cardiff. And they hated it.

I was there for about six years, but Dorothy cried so much when she had to go back to school that eventually they [their parents] allowed her to leave and sent her to a private school in Bedford. Nothing would make me cry, especially for that reason. I stuck it.

What 'that reason' was is unclear, but Marjorie was learning not to display her emotions. Self-preservation dominated, even if it meant bowing to repressive rules that no one liked. She would not be cowed by Howell's.

And so, by the age of fourteen, Marjorie had to cope with the vagaries of boarding school by herself. Though dependent on half-term visits home to her understanding father and ebullient younger brothers for reassurance and support, she was serious and studious at Howell's, surviving there until just before her eighteenth birthday.

By the first decade of the last century when Miss Kendall was in charge and Marjorie was enrolled, Howell's had grown in stature and academic competence from its precarious beginnings in 1860. Its imposing edifice built by the Howell Foundation for thirty 'orphan inmates' and thirty 'pay boarders' thrived under the extreme measures of Miss Kendall. Soon she was able to employ specialist teachers, and Howell's became one of the few girls' schools in the country to be eligible for examination by the Oxford and Cambridge Board, with the first girl from Howell's being admitted to Cambridge in 1887. The school continues to flourish and celebrated its one-hundred-and-fortieth birthday in the year 2000.

In earlier times strict discipline prevailed. During Marjorie's unhappy years there, tennis courts had been installed along with a chemistry laboratory, yet students were not allowed to speak a word as they moved from one room to another between classes. They were even punished if they spoke in the day room where they gathered before meals. Keeping a room full of young girls silent must have been a monumental task.

We were about eighty boarders and slept in dormitories according to our age. As we progressed, it happened that I ended up in the dorm for the elder girls because I was there until the coming of my eighteenth birthday – I think it was then.

16

Dr. Ieuan Thomas family, circa 1905, Marjorie fourth from left.

Jeanie and her hens, Hirwaun.

Hirwaun, Glamorgan, Wales circa 1916.

Howell's School, Llandaff, Cardiff, Wales.

Marjorie at Maesyffrwd, Hirwaun circa 1916.

Neptune fountain, Düsseldorf, Germany.

The Kaufhof department store, Düsseldorf, Germany.

Mademoiselle, Margot, Martha Blümcke, Düsseldorf, 1911.

Stadt Theatre, Weimar, Germany. Statue of Goethe and Schiller in foreground.

Former von Dürckheim-Montmartin
Royal Family schloss, Steingaden,
Germany, property of Evangelical
Church in 2000.

von Dürckheim-Montmartin Coat of Arms,
Welfenmunster, Steingaden, Germany.

Le Moulin des Ecluses, St-Jacut-de-la-Mer, France, 1912. Gabrielle and Georgette Gérard-Varet in foreground.

Marjorie in Breton costume, France, 1912.

St-Jacut-de-la-Mer, Brittany, France, 1912. Beach scene.

Pension Sablé, St-Jacut-de-la-Mer, 1912.

St-Jacut-de-la-Mer beach party of Gérard-Varet family and friends, 1912.
Marjorie second from right rear, Louis right foreground.

Picnic Cap Fréhel, 1912. Marjorie second from left, Louis fourth from left.

Swim party, St-Jacut-de-la-Mer, 1912. Louis, Gabrielle, Marjorie, friend, Georgette, Céline.

We had to get up early at half-past-six and do half an hour's study preparation or half an hour practice on violin or piano, and as I did both I was kept busy. And if you did not get this practice in, you were reported in French at night at sort of evening hymn-reading. Meals were very severe; for tea we would have great slabs of bread and butter or marg, I don't know which, and sometimes a rice pudding with grains all floating about in it. I hated this pudding so much that I used to pick up the grains one by one, and because I hadn't finished with the rest, I was put down at another table [with others who had committed misdemeanours] until I had finished, which you can imagine was an awful thing for me to have to do. We had lovely grounds, and the place was beautifully kept, but all the same it was the strictness of it. Life wasn't life there.

Years later Marjorie expressed some regrets:

I didn't do very well, but I was a fairly conscientious worker but not brilliant. I didn't over-tax my brain. I took the violin and the piano and at first was very well taught on the violin, before later getting inadequate instruction. However, I did manage to get the music prize for the whole school, which was a great surprise to me. Two beautiful volumes, one of Beethoven and one of Mozart. What I did with them, I don't know, but I'm afraid I didn't treasure them. I didn't take advantage of all that was offered me at this school. There were many good teachers there; I could have done much better. My maths were terrible; I couldn't do anything with physics, algebra, or arithmetic. The rest of my subjects were reasonable and quite good.

But it was still a shock when her matriculation results arrived in the post. There was the Junior Certificate of the Central Welsh Board awarding higher stages for English Language, History, and Botany; higher stage with distinction in Literature, a pass for Latin and for French with conversational power. No mathematics. She had failed her Welsh Matriculation and her chances for university lay in ruins.

I had a miserable time with my mother wondering what on earth I could do. I cried for hours and hours. Finally a solution was

17

found. A cousin had been to a finishing school in Germany where she was successful, so I was offered either to go to London and take a secretarial course which was to be obtained in a year's time, or to go abroad to Germany. Feeling that I would not manage the course in a year, I chose to go to Germany.

What she wanted to study at university, and which university she hoped to attend, is not spoken about. With maths and sciences being her poor subjects, she would have been unable to qualify for a school of medicine in the footsteps of her father, and in spite of all those childhood years of music training, she did not play an instrument of any kind after leaving Howell's. There was never a hint at teaching piano as her mother had done in her early days before marriage. What Marjorie did enjoy at school was French and German, both of which became her *raison d'être* for further studies abroad.

Emotionally and sexually, she now hovered on the edge of an abyss. After almost eighteen years of class-regimented development and being governed by mistresses attempting to enforce rules of self-denial, this Welsh adolescent-cum-young woman adventured without a chaperon across the Channel into Europe. And all this only five years before the Great War. Her life tumbled into unknowns: forays into foreign and exciting worlds that were different in setting and behaviour and attitudes from anything she had previously experienced.

German finishing schools would be her initiation. And luckily, there would be no higher maths to worry about as few *höhere Mädchenschulen* taught beyond basic arithmetic and possibly some geometry, since foreign languages were the most popular and most advantageous studies in these 'high schools for girls'.

Seventeen years old, almost five feet tall and weighing about seven stone, the *merch fach* (little girl) from Wales was 'very happy'.

Chapter 2

TRAVEL TO GERMANY: 1909

Travelling to Germany was the first adventure. Marjorie remembered leaving Hirwaun on the 2:15 train, sitting by herself and watching the figure of her father under his familiar black umbrella recede against the outline of the colliery winding-shed. She also remembered the dun-coloured slag heaps from the old iron works beside black coal tips from the mines as a background, and how her family's imposing home for the past few years, Maesyffrwd, 'the stream's field', rose above the endless lines of miners' slate-roof homes.

Dressed in the Edwardian fashions of high collar and long-sleeve blouse, floor-length woollen skirt, corset and bust bodice and combinations, the solo traveller laid aside her new wide-brimmed picture hat and checked her hand bag. There was a book of travel coupons, one coupon for each leg of her journey: the train to London Paddington, transfer to Victoria and on to Queenboro' dock where her steamer was scheduled to sail at quarter-past-ten that night across the Channel to Flushing Dock in Holland; and finally a continental train all the way to Düsseldorf in Germany, arriving at 11.30 the next morning. It was September, 1909, seven weeks before her eighteenth birthday, and a prelude to the apocalyptic changes that no one, least of all Marjorie, had any inkling were about to happen.

She had been to London once before, and Paddington was not unlike the central station in Cardiff, but transferring to Victoria Station with her steamer trunk was a daunting task. She hailed a porter who deposited her and her trunk in a cab with a strange gentleman; she kept her head down, remembering not to speak with strangers as her mother had so judiciously warned. When the carriage halted, the young lady from the colliery town in Wales found herself sheltered under Victoria's colossal glass canopy along with masses of humanity that hummed and circulated, running for trains, hailing cabs, disgorging mountains of baggage from incoming carriages. Newsboys screeched the day's headlines. Dark-skinned hawkers were selling the latest, absolutely thief-proof passport case. Marjorie followed as the porter threaded through the maze with her precious possessions. At last she stood under the huge banner reading 'BOAT TRAIN' to Germany and Switzerland. The porter dragged the trunk to the ticket window, stamped it 'THROUGH TO DUSSELDORF', and hoisted it onto the baggage carrier. There was no turning back.

She made her way to her seat on the train. On top in her portmanteau was the copy of *Colloquial German* that Dolly had given her as a *bon-voyage* present. Her sister's bewildered look when they said goodbye, as if she couldn't quite believe her older sister was really going off to the Continent to go to school, was not unlike Marjorie's own sense of disbelief. Now her review of German phrases and verb tenses only dimly remembered from her school studies somehow made things seem more real. Tomorrow she would be in Germany.

The night steamer was christened *'Prins Hendrick'*, an appropriately Saxon greeting. Marjorie made her way up the gangplank and followed the queue to the purser's office. A very special *bon-voyage* gift from her father had been the luxury of a single-berth cabin on the steamer for an extra ten shillings. 'You will get some sleep and arrive fresh the next day,' he had reasoned. Her mother's disapproving look didn't matter. Down the corridor from her cabin was the wireless telegraph office, and she was reminded to telegraph home, letting everyone know she was safely on board. She was amazed to think that she had almost forgotten. Home was so distant from this voyage in the night.

The churning of the ship's engines lulled gently with the sea. The Channel was a flat liquid floor, pierced by the Royal Mail Route to the Continent. Images from long ago, when she was no more than three years old, floated to the surface. She remembered the passageway at Tyclyd:

> I had come jumping out of the dining room into the hall, but stopped in my tracks at the sight of my parents, Mother sitting

at the bottom of the stairs dressed in a yellow satin ball-gown, weeping. Father was bending over, coaxing Mother to stop crying and go with him to whatever affair they were going to. Then I knew they were my parents, but it was the first time I was aware of them, or of anywhere around me being my home. What happened afterwards I don't know.

Marjorie related these incidents several times in the last few years of her life – both being on the ship and recurring visions of her three-year-old awareness. Both were significant: sailing to Germany meant freedom but consciousness of home and parents was not completely suppressed.

The steward's knock with his tea-and-biscuit breakfast woke everyone in time to disembark at Flushing dock at five o'clock. Sleepy passengers shuffled onto the train: direction 'The Rhine', final destination 'Basle, Switzerland'. Customs control was at Goch where all baggage was cleared, whilst everyone stood by their own trunks. It didn't take long, and at 11:30 a colourful sign announced the Hauptbahnhof of Düsseldorf. In less than twenty-four hours Marjorie had travelled by herself from a colliery town in Wales across the English Channel to an elegant German city on the Rhine. A different language, strange money, electric trams on wide boulevards, shops more fashionable than London, and everyone saying *guten morgen* to everyone, even strangers in the street. How would she ever describe this scene to those at home?

Chapter 3

School in Düsseldorf: 1909

Marjorie spoke about her first day, and how she cautiously parted the lace curtains in the dining-room window to investigate when the bells rang again. They had been clanging every fifteen minutes since she had first awoken, and now she realized they were coming from nearby in the street. Just as she looked out, the Number Eight tram turned into the boulevard at the corner, ringing its bell. Behind her, other students entered, their laughter suspended, she could tell. She hoped it was because they didn't want to startle the new English-speaking girl.

Christel, the oldest, glanced out of the window at the clanging tram, and explained to a bewildered Marjorie. The tram was to go shopping at the *Kaufhof*, the big store, but Marjorie didn't understand. She had never been shopping, let alone on a tram.

But within days she would accompany the German girls on the *strassenbahn* to the Königsallee where there were parks and a fountain called Neptune who spit water out of his mouth. The girls' carefree independence stunned Marjorie at first, but she quickly learned that she had to get used to everyone chatting at once at breakfast while slices of rye bread with meat and cheese disappeared. Then there was a final taste of raspberry preserves (which Marjorie never forgot), a cup of coffee, and everyone was whisked into the classroom. This breakfast was a far cry from the silent tea-and-porridge routine of the past, so far away in Wales. And her German was no match for theirs – yet. She wondered how this Neptune spat water. Should she take her umbrella if she did go?

Fortunately, it didn't take long. She remembers with relief that within a week she was conversing, at least in the classroom. In the adjoining *pensionat* where they lived, two girls to a room, there was a continuous hubbub of young ladies' hustle and bustle

22

and 'I [Marjorie] was often in the middle.' What she wanted to say in German, the others wanted to speak in English. Usually it was a confusion of both languages echoing down from the high ceilings. Mademoiselle, the French teacher from Alsace on the Germany/France border, chaperoned their outings and was easily persuaded to go wherever the girls directed. The *Kaufhof* would be everyone's first foray into the city.

The tram wasn't too alarming, if one knew where one was going. It was like riding a fast-moving train for short distances. Marjorie paid close attention to street names and tram numbers. She was on the Number Eight on Goethe Strasse before turning onto the Königsallee. The *Kaufhof* was a gigantic department store, built in the modern Jugendstil Art Nouveau style where columns of windows three stories high graced the façade and were capped with copper railings which matched the copper roof. One could buy everything one needed or wanted for one's whole life here, it seemed. There were other small shops, but the *Kaufhof* was Düsseldorf's crowning glory.

After the Königsallee and then the English-style Hofgarten park with more spitting fountains, Marjorie was able to laugh – at her umbrella, her old fears, her hesitant German. Nothing was going to harm her in this majestic city, and she wasn't punished for saying street instead of *strasse*.

There was one more stop. The new 'English' girl from Wales must have some German beer along with a *Wurst* sausage. The best place was next to the theatre in the Hofgarten, and to everyone's delight, the beer garden was serving outside on this sun-filled autumn day. Beer was totally foreign to Marjorie, but after a few sips to wash down the fat, white sausage (made from baby cows they said), she remembered that it was all delicious. It was now just a month away from Marjorie's eighteenth birthday. How many more transformations would she experience before then?

No doubt there were many. Margot, along with Christel and Martha Blümcke became life-long friends. Their school terms were separated by exhilarating holidays at Christel and Martha's home at Weilburg near Koblenz. For Marjorie, these days were some of the happiest times of her life. Her unexpected but relished new-found freedom allowed her to travel with her friends by boat up-river beyond Koblenz, past the famous castles and through the Rhine Gorge, where the Lorelei lured unsuspecting sailors to their doom, and dared innocent school girls to explore the secrets of the Rhine.

In spite of the lures of local legends, cities like Bonn, Beethoven's birthplace, beckoned. The immense Dom cathedral at Cologne was Marjorie's first glimpse into the religious intensity of a Catholic pilgrimage site, its massive Gothic structure combining medieval with nineteenth-century romantics in its shrines and spires and stained glass. In the *Marktplatz* of Weilburg another *Neptunbrunnen* ('Neptune fountain') spouted water at her. Dim memories of earlier school music stories from the *Nibelungenlied* and Wagner's operas came to life. For Marjorie's part, there was no end to her stories about growing up in a Welsh coal-mining town along with tales from her strict girls' boarding school where 'life wasn't life'.

'Let me tell you about,' she would begin in English, until everyone was giggling at rice pudding kernels desecrated in German. But the German girls were sobered by the severity of the school rules: how the students were punished if they spoke while changing classrooms or while waiting to be served their meals, and how Marjorie was reprimanded before the whole school if she failed to do her music. Most of all they liked the stories about her home: how she walked three miles every Saturday to Aberdare to her violin lesson, toting an instrument case her eight-year-old hands could barely carry, before scrambling another one and a half miles uphill to catch a train home, her solace being two pence for a pound of dates devoured while waiting for the train. 'Where the stones went, I don't know,' she writes decades later.

October 27 was birthday-time. Marjorie was eighteen; Christel would be nineteen in another week. *Das Rheingold* was being performed at the Hofgarten Theatre and Mademoiselle was able to get tickets. The whole class attended the performance: gnomes and gold rings and fairies of the Rhine reflected on the castle of Valhalla where greed and curses triumphed in the end. Marjorie wanted redemption, or at least the Ring to be restored to its rightful owners, but mythology reigned. She would have to wait for the next instalments for the Rhine to flow with gold again. When they stopped at the beer garden after the opera, a happy *prost* (cheers!) and *Herzliche Glückwünschen* (congratulations) were raised to the Welsh and German birthday girls. Such a birthday Marjorie had never imagined. But secretly, no matter how she tried, she never really acquired a taste for their beer; she found the sweet Mosel wine more palatable.

On her pillow at the *pensionat* was a small gift from Margot. Marjorie slipped the ribbon and tissue off to hold a treasure she would keep for many years: a miniature girl reading a book, so adroitly crafted by a German ceramist.

Birthday greetings arrived from home. Her brothers' scrawl on the postcards made her smile. A pang of homesickness pricked her conscience. Geoffrey, three years younger than Marjorie, was no doubt proud of his emphatic heavy-nibbed signature. He included the scores from his season's football championships, the only important news for him. The others just said 'Happy Birthday,' as if they were at a loss for words to the stranger in their family. Marjorie tried to respond by describing the opera but after two attempts she simply said that it was 'a wonderful performance.' She couldn't envisage that they could imagine her description of gold rings in the great river and fairies and gnomes flitting about a castle. For Marjorie, Shakespeare's Oberon and Titania and Puck were no match for Wagner's Nibelungs at Valhalla.

Weihnachten 1913 ('Christmas 1913') is written on the back of a faded photograph. The picture is taken at Vielbach, the Blümcke family home. Snow blankets everything, even the cart being hauled over the bridge across the brook. Electrical wires stretch between tall poles, plumb-line straight, bringing cheer to the Christmas scene where Marjorie spent the festive holidays of both 1909 and 1910. Christmas trees decorated with candles and spice cookies; carol-singing at the church in the snow; a fat goose for the holiday feast; small gifts – a candle or ornament – from the local market. This was Christmas in Rhineland.

Her last extant communication with the Blümckes is in 1968 in postcards carefully preserved with her papers. But their friendship was mentioned only occasionally to her family. No other contact with her Düsseldorf school friends took place after her years in Germany, and there is no mention of particular friendships from Weimar where she continued at school the following year. However, the warmth of the Düsseldorf welcome, along with the foreign travels and language, had liberated the 'squashed' young woman of just a few months before. Such affection and acceptance inspired unexpected confidence and independence in Marjorie, provoking a desire to master the German language still further.

Chapter 4

WEIMAR: 1910 TO 1911

'We enjoy what is old, but we are driven by our intellect to create what is new.'

motto of the New Weimar Society
founded by Franz Liszt and friends in 1854

How Marjorie came to be at Weimar for her second year of study is not known, but the most probable explanation is on the recommendation of her language teachers. After her summer holiday along the Rhine, a train journey of about 225 kilometres eastward through rolling woodlands took her to the middle of Thuringia, the heart of ancient Germany. There she would have found a smaller city than Düsseldorf, but the same modern electric trams in broad avenues, *konditorei* for fancy cakes, and a wonderland of opera.

Her notes tell us:

The next year I went to a finishing school in Weimar to teach English and become proficient in German. I'm afraid my part of the bargain was not as good as it should have been, but we had fun – such as sneaking out at night when the girls were in bed and bringing back a big bag of doughnuts, just escaping getting into trouble for my misdeeds. The school was housed in the *Schiller Haus* – a beautiful old house in which I was proud to live. Schiller the idealist had really lived in the house. Goethe the realist had also lived in Weimar for some time; so had Liszt. There is a statue of Schiller and Goethe in front of the *Stadt* theatre in Weimar. The school often went to the theatre to hear operas – *Lohengrin, Tannhäuser, the Magic Flute, Undine*, etc. It was a happy carefree life.

I had the misfortune to lose my money on the way back to school after spending Christmas at my other school friend's home [the Blümcke's at Vielbach near Weilburg]. Not wanting to write home for money, I asked the Headmistress if she would allow me to give English lessons in the town – Weimar was a garrison town – and I was soon using my free time giving lessons to the daughters of two of the soldiers – Graf von Dürckheim and Baron (I've forgotten his name) who were related. During the summer vacation the family would transfer itself – tutors, governesses, man and maid servants – to their castle at Steingaden near Garmisch in Bavaria. I went with them. This was in 1911 – a glorious summer in a glorious part of the world.

Weimar had been the seat of the German Enlightenment in the eighteenth century. A compact country town, it remains a stately centre for the German people, whose historic national culture is as alive today as three centuries ago. In Johann Wolfgang von Goethe's time (1749 – 1832), it was known as 'the Athens of the North'. Goethe and his friend, Friedrich Schiller (1759 - 1805), were Europe's leading literary figures, with their respective *Faust* and *William Tell* revealing their philosophies in poetry and drama. Love triumphant, evil conquered, and patriotism subduing tyranny were their inspiring themes, anticipating the French Revolution and the reshaping of Europe in the following century. Ironically, the Enlightenment came full circle another hundred years later in the Weimar Republic, the post-war government of 1919 that died within fifteen years of its inception, its democratic ideals unable to survive the fascism empowered by Hitler's mighty army.

Just as with Shakespeare, Goethe and Schiller's stories continue to be re-told in contemporary opera and theatre, as tantalizing and challenging now as they would have been for Marjorie when she was a young adult in Weimar. Even in her ninetieth year she continued to ponder over Goethe's realism, especially in *Faust*, where she recalled that 'Mephistopheles wasn't a very realistic devil, not like Schiller's William Tell who rose up against his enemies.'

Today both Goethe and Schiller are immortalized, larger than life, together holding a laurel wreath in Weimar's Theaterplatz. The *Stadt* theatre has been rebuilt following the Allied bombing of its auditorium in a massive air raid in February, 1945, but the Greek-style columnar façade is the original built in 1909, a year before Marjorie's arrival. Attending the operas must have been intoxicating, with the lavish productions and romantic muses of Mozart and Wagner vying for attention, flirting with the impressionable young students. Marjorie's recollection of *Undine* is illuminating. It is an obscure opera, rarely performed today, and is based on the popular premise of a water nymph falling in love with a human, not unlike Hans Christian Andersen's *Little Mermaid*. It is a story of adolescent awakening and separation from family, very similar to Marjorie's, which is perhaps why she remembered it so many years later.

Her school in a *Schiller Haus* could have been in one of several places home to the Schiller family in the late eighteenth century. The house where he spent the final few years of his life has been a Schiller Museum since the 1840s; the 'Yellow House' on Windischenstrasse behind the Museum was an earlier Schiller address which could have housed classrooms in 1910, but Weimar city records show that it was an office for paying school fees. City records also disclose only two *höhere Töchterschulen* (literal translation 'higher daughter's schools') in Weimar in 1910. The *Sophienstift* was founded in 1878 by Countess Sophie Grossherzogin for daughters of higher standing or class, instituting scholarship beyond the usual governess level available at that time. The other school on record is labelled simply *Höhere Privat-Mädchenschule* ('Private Girl's High school') located in today's Washingtonstrasse, a nondescript street where Schiller may have lived at one time. Its listed faculty had seven names plus an arch deacon. *Sophienstift* had thirteen faculty members plus several professors and doctors of philosophy which no doubt places the school fees and its upper class of pupils beyond Marjorie's realm, both financially and socially. It is difficult to imagine any other English students at either school. Marjorie must have been unique as Weimar was a provincial centre for Germanic culture and education whereas Düsseldorf was a well-known destination on the Rhine for the many British who exchanged places with German tourists. In Weimar, like Liszt fifty years before, she was creating something new, at least for her intellect.

The *Privat-Mädchenschule* in Washingtonstrasse was only a few blocks from the *Stadt* theatre. The Hofkonditorie Weiner Café and the Kaiser Kaffee, both on Schillerstrasse, offered a convenient rendezvous for midnight doughnut-raids and the necessary bribes to keep the revels of rebellious classmates a secret. Marjorie would not have been alone as she tiptoed across forbidden thresholds, but each act of defiance was to her an act of personal discovery. A circular route back to the school passed through the market square with its familiar Neptune fountain across from the Elephant Inn, an institute of hospitality since the sixteenth century. Marjorie remembered creeping past the *Weinstube* (wine bar) with her innocent 'ladies-of-the-night' accompanied by the accordion and zither strains that drifted into their shadows.

This was the Weimar of history, culture and art. The Weimar of English-style parks with statues, including one of Shakespeare, where Renaissance, neo-Gothic and classical architecture stood side by side with modern *Jugendstil*. The Weimar, above all where the famous names of Goethe, Schiller, Liszt, Richard Strauss, J. S. Bach, Richard Wagner, Napoleon and Nietzsche seeped out of the buildings and operatic settings. It is easy to see how these combined to create a profound rite of passage for the nineteen-year-old Welsh girl from the coal mines of the Cynon Valley.

Her remembrance so many years later of Schiller and Goethe reflects her impressions at the time; how trying to understand the philosophies of the German Enlightenment helped her to understand her own discoveries and answer some of her own questions. What kind of world did she fit into now that she was fluent in German and had lived in its culture, one that was so alien from, and so often disapproved of, by her own? She knew she was happy in Germany with its ancient castles and timeless operas, its foreign philosophies, its new friendships. And she knew she didn't want to go home. Surreptitiously, she began to investigate further studies abroad.

Another finishing school alumna from Weimar was the actress Marlene Dietrich whose father was in the Royal Prussian Police and most likely stationed in Weimar. Marlene was born ten years after Marjorie and was possibly a student at *Sophienstift* which did not become a public school until 1917. Marlene would have been sixteen by then and studying to become a concert violinist. However, a muscle injury to her arm forced her to abandon that hope, and it was a German poet that she read while in Weimar that inspired her to become an actress. Indeed, when she recited one of his poems at the audition for her first film role, she got the part. But the havoc created by war would soon force Marlene and Marjorie to see beyond the poetic.

Marlene left Germany, pursued her acting career, and became an American citizen. When she returned to her native Berlin in 1960, her one-woman show was a sell-out. The standing ovations she received suggested a nation's sympathy for her assertion that 'You can't reject your whole upbringing. But I just could not endure the turn my country took.' Unlike Marjorie, she was able to return to her homeland with her foreign experiences a measure of her success. In the early twentieth century Marlene's movie and cabaret performances gave her worldwide acclaim, while Marjorie taught English to keep herself within the confines of Europe, albeit temporarily. When she did go home several years later, her experiences abroad were shared with no one beyond her family. She would return to the Continent for holidays, but only to the French coast of Brittany and Normandy with her father and occasionally some girl friends. She never revisited the Rhineland or the home of the German Enlightenment that had brought her own enlightenment.

When she lost her money, another chapter unfolded. As the German aristocracy did not completely collapse until the title and land reforms of 1931, in 1910 Counts and Barons flourished, especially in garrison towns such as Weimar. When Marjorie first brought her valuable English skills to their children, the Count von Dürckheim-Montmartin family probably lived in military quarters like the Royal Stables near the Palace which had been completed in 1878. The von Dürckheim *Jugendstil* palace on Cranach Strasse was not built until 1913 which is beyond Marjorie's time, so exactly where she first knew the family in Weimar is not known. But their annual summer trek to Steingaden was to the property of the Royal Family of

31

Dürckheim-Montmartin, a beautiful country home in the foothills of the Bavarian Alps in the Five Lakes region known as the *Pfaffenwinkel* which means 'Cleric's Corner' because of the numerous churches and monasteries in the area.

The *schloss* in Steingaden dates from 1845 when the Countess Alexandrine built the villa for her heirs whose title passed from King Ludwig II of Bavaria, a descendant of the Palatine Counts who wrested Protestant Germany from the clutches of the Holy Roman Empire way back in the sixteenth century. Best remembered for his flight of fancy in the Disneyesque castle at Neuschwanstein begun in 1869 and never finished, Ludwig is also noted for the mad extravagance of another fanciful castle built as a replica of Versailles on an island in Lake Chiemsee in 1885, just before his mysterious death purportedly by drowning in a lake close to Steingaden. His legacy – apart from madness and architectural monstrosities – was the continuation of the autonomous kingdom-state of Bavaria which remained outside mainstream Germany until it finally succumbed to the restructuring of West Germany following World War II. The Bavaria of today, home of fashionable Munich, beer festivals and ski chalets in the Alps, boasts thousands of tourists who recall the wonder of the Hall of Mirrors at Chiemsee that reflect the one week that Ludwig lived there.

Marjorie's castle was not so elaborate; in fact it was a modest villa, but referred to as the *schloss* ('castle' or 'palace') by the local people. Not only did the von Dürckheim-Montmartins own the *schloss* with its large garden and over one hundred hectares of farmland, but the local brewery and dairy belonged to them as well. In 1897 Countess Alexandrine's younger son, Count Friedrich, had to pay his mother 400,000 goldmarks to purchase the *schloss* for his family. The year before, he had acquired a logging operation with its large lands along with other smaller properties around the *schloss*, and he married Countess Charlotte von Kusserow reputedly of a noble Russian family but born in Berlin, and the bearer of a dowry of five million goldmarks to her marriage.

Children born of this marriage were son Wolf Heinrich in 1900, daughter Isa in 1897, son Karlfried in 1896, son Wilfried in 1902, and youngest daughter Antonia who was still alive in

Portrait photo of Marjorie taken for Louis, circa 1913.

Afernoon tea at Madame Sablé's boarding house, Rennes, France 1912. Marjorie in centre.

M. Louis Gérard-Varet, Rector, University of Rennes, France, circa 1910.

Rector Gérard-Varet greeting President Poincaré of France at Rennes, France 1913.

Statue of Anatole Le Braz and Margaret Philippe at St. Brieuc,
Brittany, France.

Museum of Rennes, France, circa 1913. Top floor is Gérard-Varet family
apartment. Marjorie's room is marked with a box around the window
in centre.

Boys' School, Rennes, France circa 1914 when it became a Military Hospital.

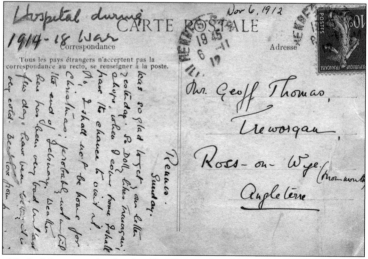

Marjorie's postcard to brother Geoffrey saying 'No, I shall not be home for Christmas.' Date is December, 1912 and she is staying in France with Louis and family for the holidays.

Photo portrait of Princess Aymon de Faucigny Lucinge, 'Souvenir of the War', 1914-1915.

Marjorie amongst hospital personnel observing awarding of Military Cross to patient from hospital.

Staff, Rennes Military Hospital, France, 1914.
Marjorie third from left first row standing; Céline, sixth from left first row
standing; Princess Lucinge eighth from left first row standing; Duchess de
Rohan seated in front on right.

Marjorie, friend, Céline, Princess
Lucinge at Rennes Military
Hospital, 1914

International trio of war: Zouave,
Moroccan, French soldiers, all
patients of Marjorie's.

Souvenir of the war: drawing of farm scene by Belgian patient
A. de Saint Jean.

Patients and nursing staff, Hospital Stell-Tuck, Rueil-Malmaison, France,
1915. Princess Lucinge on left; Marjorie in centre.

Souvenir of the war: drawing with camel motif by Zouave patient
Ozary 2039.

2000. This chronology is taken from the mausoleum built for the family complete with their coat of arms embedded in its wall and located in the churchyard of the *Welfenmunster*, Steingaden's rare Romanesque church and former monastery with its famous ceiling frescoes almost six hundred years old. Marjorie did not remember these bits of history from the small sub-alpine village not much larger than Hirwaun, but she stood in awe before the towering mountains when the entourage left the train for their waiting carriage in Füssen. Meandering along the River Lech to the *schloss* up in the woods above the town square and church, sipping a cool glass of Steingaden beer and calling to the scampering children in English to remind them of their lessons transformed her two-month working holiday. She remembered that 'glorious warm summer' of picnics and swim parties when everyone cooled off in the lakes nestled in the rambling hills, English lessons an incidental accompaniment. Marjorie taught two daughters of related families: Isa von Dürckheim-Montmartin who was thirteen years old at the time, and perhaps a daughter of the Montmartin side who may be present in the photo taken two years before at Steingaden. No doubt younger daughter Antonia, called 'Tony', also acquired some English expressions to add to her six-year-old vocabulary.

The family photograph was reproduced in a Weimar newspaper story concerning the 1990 restoration of the von Dürckheim Palace in Weimar, so grandly built in 1913 and so ungraciously barricaded when it became the headquarters of the East German STASI secret police from 1950 to 1989. In the years between 1927 and 1932 in land reforms initiated by the Weimar Republic, all royal property was forcibly sold, mostly at low prices under the hammer of an auctioneer, and the funds deposited in the German Central Credit Bank in Berlin. The nobility lost everything of value. Countess Charlotte began in 1927 to give ownership of the properties in the community to those who were living in them. By 1931 son Karlfried, now a Professor, lost many battles with the authorities in his efforts to save the *schloss* at Steingaden. With the loss of their home, the von Dürckheim-Montmartins left Steingaden and the *schloss* was unoccupied for six years. Since then it has been a headquarters for American occupying forces, an old people's home, and was finally sold to the Evangelical Church who now use it as a conference centre and rural retreat. Its idyllic setting has been maintained in spite of its changing façades, but carefree children's voices are just whispers in the cooling breezes.

The newspaper article also describes the original occupants of the Weimar palace:

> Countess Charlotte was a vivacious, highly intelligent and pleasant woman very interested in the arts. The atmosphere in the house was very free and informal and described as highly intellectual . . . Wilfried and his younger brother and sister took piano lessons . . . the Inner Circle of guests included the Director of Music at the Stadt Theatre, a sculptor, a painter and illustrator, and the famous pianist Bernhard Stavenhagen.

In another article about the family, Count Friedrich is "a jovial, charming, youthful fifty year old, very natural and relaxed and without conceit". It was a carefree time for Marjorie with a happy, outgoing family wanting her company on their summer holiday.

She doesn't want the 'glorious summer' to end, but at the beginning of October she receives a postcard in Steingaden from Martha in Düsseldorf asking about future plans, and speculating enigmatically: "Money, what is that after all?" Marjorie has arranged for her European pursuits to continue. She now has the opportunity to stretch her two years abroad into a third, having been accepted in a Diploma for Foreigners programme at the University of Rennes in France. But will her father protest?

Chapter 5

HIRWAUN, WALES: CHRISTMAS 1911

At the end of October Marjorie once again finds herself at the home of Martha and Christel Blümcke at Weilburg. Margot also comes along for a grand reunion before the four young women separate forever, some continuing studies in Düsseldorf, and Marjorie moving on to France. They each believe they will see each other again soon and that their close bonds will never be broken. Marjorie's twentieth birthday is celebrated with her favourite Riesling from a vineyard they visit in the Mosel Valley.

Down the Rhine to Düsseldorf they sail, past the soaring steeples of Köln's Dom and only metres away from foaming steins raised in *prosts* on the over-hanging balconies of half-timbered burghers' houses hugging the river banks. These last impressions of Germany crystallize the good times for Marjorie – the beer and *wurst* at her Hofgarten birthday party; Niebelungs finally rescuing the gold ring; *Weihnacten* with her dear friends at Weilburg; the theatreplatz in Weimar and her Schiller-house school; swim parties from the schloss at Steingaden – all drifting memories now mixed with tearful goodbyes. When a porter shifts her steamer trunk to the waiting railway carriage, she notices how the newly acquired labels from Düsseldorf, Weimar, Füssen, and Weilburg announce her itinerary to the world. She is exposed. Everyone who 'reads' her trunk will know she has travelled, and can probably speak some German, but only she knows her inner secret, her intrepid pursuit of further unknowns. In spite of her sad *auf wiedersehens*, a smile steals across her face when it is gently touched by cool rain drops while she waits on the platform, picture hat in hand. The magic summer of 1911 is slipping away, into a new season in another country, again across the Channel from home.

First there is the Boat Train to London. This time it is a rough crossing, and there is not the luxury of a private cabin, but Marjorie is becoming a seasoned traveller who enjoys mingling with other passengers. The Ladies' Lounge is furnished with settees and foot stools and travel rugs, all attended by an English maid who brings tea and biscuits just as the ship begins to heave in all directions. No one drinks the tea or has a biscuit, hoping abstinence is the best treatment for *mal de mer*. Everyone concentrates on not filling their sea-sickness bag. The scheduled eight-hour journey stretches into a nine-and-a-half one before the ship reaches calm water, giving just enough time for Marjorie to grasp that she is now nearing Britain and home for the first time in two years. Of course she is older and wiser, but the real change is her exuberance and laughter. She has discovered that life can be fun, that she can make friends, and that Europe is filled with wonderful sites.

That afternoon she is home in Hirwaun. Her brothers stare; sister Dorothy is away at school; mother Jeanie is tight-lipped as usual; father Ieuan is full of questions. 'How was your crossing? Tell us about the schloss . . . What did you eat at school? Speak some German to us . . .'

'Guten Abend mein Vater. Die Reise mit das Schiff war ganz sturmisch und wir waren seekrank.' ('Good evening Father. My journey on the ship was very stormy, and we were seasick.') Demonstrating using the seasick bag makes her brothers laugh; Jeanie rings for the maid to bring tea. Soon it is time for bed before everyone collapses under the excitement of the eldest daughter's homecoming. Jeanie remains impassive, reminding us that as the government-appointed School's Inquiry Commission of 1868 claimed: 'The finishing school is not so much an educational agent as a tribute which the parent pays to his own social position.' Marjorie's new role is unsettling. She has not envisioned being ignored by her mother, who casts aside her daughter's European escapades, as if they have no consequence.

Dorothy returned from her teachers' training college at Ambleside in Cumbria for the Christmas holidays, along with Geoffrey who was given leave from his farm studies in

Herefordshire. Together with Marjorie, the three older siblings were a party of strangers until they shared their escapades, telling tales of freedom: Marjorie sneaking out for doughnuts in that far-away German town; Dorothy going to the cinema and meeting boys from the school across the road; and Geoff being chased by a bull after he forgot to close a gate. Ben, aged fifteen and Glyn, aged thirteen were spellbound as well as honour-bound not to repeat the stories to their parents. Marjorie felt a renewed closeness with Geoff who had always been her favourite. Dorothy was still in a world of her own, struggling to leave adolescence behind, but more interested in boys than other-world adventures.

Jeanie was nonplussed by her growing family. They no longer required her management, and indeed rejected her interference. Glyn was convinced he could emulate Geoff and stay up late, until he fell asleep curled at Marjorie's feet in front of the fire. Ieuan was bemused and perplexed. When he didn't appear for the midday meal on Christmas Eve, everyone was suspicious of 'Mrs Jones, the Lamb', a kind publican (and patient) who had been known to ply the doctor too freely with whisky when he had been on a shoot. He was a keen marksman and rarely missed an opportunity. The day before Christmas dawned cold and clear, and it seemed a good time to break away from the noise and commotion at Maesyffrwd. When he did reappear in top voice singing 'Oh where is my wandering boy tonight, the boy of my tenderest cares,' Jeanie didn't offer tender care or join in the joke. What was going to happen next?

Christmas Day was lively with all the children home for a change. There were special gifts from Germany: hand-dipped candles for mother and sister; miniature mechanized wagons for the boys; and a tiny bicycle with turning wheels for father. Ieuan surprised Marjorie with a Brownie box camera. He had decided her escapades were worth recording for posterity but little did he suspect how long the mementoes would survive.

The whole family went to church and then came home to Christmas Dinner with Uncle Edgar and Aunt Maud. The children were asked to entertain themselves quietly. Marjorie recalled her giggles when Martha had showed her how to jump, then lie and make an angel in virgin snow at Vielbach after church on Christmas Eve. She could almost smell the steaming hot chocolate for dipping the *Lebkuchen*, and feel the melted cookie dripping on her chin. She had been young and playful and happy then. When she looked in the hall mirror at Maesyffrwd, she saw a woman too sober, too good, too quiet. It was time to go to France.

Ieuan had agreed to the tuition at Rennes. It wasn't much more than the six pounds sterling that each year had cost in Germany. Her living expenses would be more in France, but she had searched the lists until she found an affordable boarding house to which Ieuan also agreed. Hopefully she might earn some extra by teaching English.

Chapter 6

SCHOOL IN RENNES, FRANCE: 1912

January storms held true to their reputation and the ten-hour sailing from Southampton to St. Malo in 1912 seemed to take forever. Marjorie learned to eat small amounts of biscuits before and during Channel crossings; nevertheless she developed a strong aversion to the possibility of seasickness. Years later she would decline any offer of travelling to the Continent if there were even a hint of foul weather. And since high winds and rough seas are never far away from the English Channel, she did not cross after 1925. But between 1912 and 1925 she zigzagged to and from France at least six times, so she must have acquired some sea tolerance, even if only a temporary one.

After Marjorie's sixteen-hour journey from Hirwaun, the ship docked at the terminus of St. Malo's rail line. Customs was quick and before Marjorie could acclimatize to steady ground underfoot and breakfast of coffee and croissants, she was in Rennes. *'Bonjour mademoiselle'* replaced *'guten morgen'* without a blink for everyone else travelling; for Marjorie there was a difference. The French were so fast, abrupt, and matter-of-fact. *'Suivez-moi, suivez-moi'* repeated the porter as he charged up the street pulling her trunk on a cart, Madame Sablé's address in hand.

Madame Sablé, a widow, ran a boarding house for female students studying at the University of Rennes. There were five French girls and Marjorie, two to a room, a large bath and separate toilet room shared by all. Breakfast was bowls of coffee or chocolate accompanied by croissants and *pain au chocolat*, tantalizing pastry filled with chocolate that quickly became irresistible. Lunch was the thin slices of ham, sausage, and cheese that Germans ate for breakfast; dinner was casserole of chicken in cider or red wine, or pork cooked in cream with dried fruits, or fish with spicy tomato sauce; then a sugared *galette* for dessert – all so exotic compared to Wales and Germany, but so wonderfully delicious. Marjorie would have to be careful, or her slim waist supported by stays in her skirts would expand and the raised waistbands, current fashion for accentuating slim figures, would have to be adjusted.

Though Marjorie's congenial friendliness gave her an equal place amongst the French students, she missed the cheery camaraderie of her German friends. When Eulalie, the Algerian cook, got 'the stunks' (a Scots term noted by Marjorie meaning to sulk, or go into a huff) and disappeared for a day, Marjorie was glad to help in the kitchen, learning new skills of Breton cuisine to accompany her growing fluency in French. Soon she discovered that her lilting Welsh accent was almost identical to that of the Bretons whose Celtic origins she shared.

Rennes is the capital of the Breton department of Ille et Vilaine where two rivers meet and serve as the gateway to Brittany and the west for the rest of France. Its two universities mark an important place for Breton as well as French scholarship. In October 1911 the Faculty of Letters of the University of Rennes moved from its premises in what is now the Museum of Rennes on the banks of the River Vilaine to a new campus, sharing its classical quadrangle with the municipal as well as the university libraries. Tucked under the arches that gracefully surround the inner courtyard of the quadrangle is a plaque commemorating the move and listing amongst other dignitaries M. Gérard-Varet, Recteur de l'Acadèmie. At the austere yet elegant building that became Marjorie's learning centre for both terms in 1912, this Rector, Monsieur Louis Gérard-Varet, would prove a valuable ally.

Ravaging fires have taken their toll on Rennes, most notably in 1720 and 1994. In 1720 the fire burned for a week, destroying most of the medieval houses, but encouraging modern rebuilding of broad rectangular streets designed by Gabriel whose son carried the ideas further to the wide boulevards around the Place de la Concorde in Paris. Rennes became a miniature Paris, classical and cultured with its theatres and museums, and lively and entertaining enough to cater for shoppers and the yearly influx of students who today number approximately forty thousand.

The fire in 1994 badly damaged the Palace of Justice, home of the Parliament of Brittany since the sixteenth century. There are many stories about the old Parliament with its 120 councillors paying high prices for their inherited seats but receiving low salaries paid in sweetmeats and spices. However, their exemption from paying taxes and power over lawyers and the law courts more than compensated for low wages! Regardless of old tales of intrigue and political fraud, today's Parliament remains a symbol of Breton independence along with the alliance with France cemented by the marriage of Duchess Anne of Brittany to Charles VIII on December 6, 1491. In present day Rennes, tradition continues beside modern stores and factories and institutions.

Although the student population of 1912 was considerably less than that in 2001, according to Marjorie she was not the only English-speaking student since she spoke about the University's "Diploma for Foreigners" programme, designed for those whose first language was not French. However, her carefully preserved parchment simply awards her a *Diplôme de Langue Française*. She must have achieved a high standing, as her professors encouraged her to further her studies. After conferring with her father, she was allowed to continue with a second term, concentrating on French literature to complement her Diploma in French Language. And Madame Sablé offered a job for the summer.

In exchange for twenty-five francs, Marjorie could have room and board if she helped with housekeeping and serving in the dining-room of Madame's summer hotel, Pension de Famille Sablé, at St-Jacut-de-la-Mer, a small fishing and seaside holiday village on the Channel's Côtes-d'Amour, approximately eighty kilometres northwest of Rennes. Marjorie did not need long to make her decision. A few weeks later together with Eulalie and Madame, the entourage set out for another grand summer for Marjorie, one she would not forget, not ever.

Chapter 7

St-Jacut-de-la-Mer: Summer 1912

Four-hundred-and-sixty years after Christ was born, Jacut, a monk from Ireland, founded a Christian monastery on the slim peninsula that juts into a large bay of the *Côte d'Émeraude* section of the *Côte d'Amour* on the north Brittany coast. More than fifteen hundred years later the monk's *Abbaye* continues to be part of what is now Saint Jacut, a small but important fishing village and just as important seaside resort. In addition to its thriving mussel and oyster farms, St-Jacut boasts fine beaches, long walks, and many picturesque points from which to view the emerald waters and islands off the 'Coast of Love'. Romance hangs in the air and blows over the sand dunes. Idling away a summer afternoon in a small craft on the calm bay, with just enough breeze to fill a dinghy sail, is a popular pastime, just as it was in 1912.

Marjorie's collection of postcard photos from her summer at St-Jacut are a record of beach scenes in the fashions of the day – women in floor-length skirts and men wearing dark three-piece suits, regardless of the heat and sand. The ladies are shielded from the sun by elaborate broad-brimmed hats tied under their chin with voluminous scarves; mothers are doing needlework while keeping an eye on children digging sand castles. *Cabines* line the seashore and towels hang to dry between their miniature frames. It is an idyllic scene, one that belies the excitement and the unexpected discoveries at the seashore for the little girl from Wales, but also one that many years later would open a path into those vulnerable days so far away and long ago.

Decades after that idyllic summer, while sifting through her collection of postcards and yellowed photographs (compliments of her father's 1911 Christmas gift), Marjorie remembered the blistering hot sand that urged her along with her group of swimmers into the sea. There they were, photographed in their dark serge swimming dresses, and as they splashed through the surf, her recollections revived. She opened a large brown envelope and carefully extracted two similar photos of herself in formal portrait poses both taken by B. Owen, Merthyr Tydfil, probably in 1913. One portrait is demure, her eyes looking down; the other is more challenging, her focus straight forward. 'These were for Louis. We met at St-Jacut.'

Which likeness she gave to Louis, she didn't say. But she did reveal, with tears in her now dimly-sighted eyes, other details about her grand summer of 1912 at St-Jacut-de-la-Mer, and falling in love.

When Louis swam alongside, her whole body tingled. Their arms touched, his lips brushed her forehead. They surfaced, swam apart, separated by invisible chaperones. For Marjorie there was a protocol she thought she had understood, the one that dictated self-preservation and denial of sensual feelings, especially anything to do with sex. Marriage was never discussed except as make-believe, a fantasy that became reality by accident. But this awakening, this touching, this heart-racing effect, this Louis . . . the joy, the laughs, the sun-burned noses, the family picnics on Cap Fréhel . . . everyone in holiday mode with Marjorie and Louis in their own exclusive utopia . . . it all seemed to carry a tinge of truth.

They walked and talked and swam. They explored each other's languages; Louis learned about Wales, Marjorie learned about France. They laughed over Marjorie's hated rice pudding at school and Louis's dread of science laboratories. They planned romantic trips on the Rhine and the Danube, waltzing in Vienna, and Christmas at Weilbach. Marjorie remembered her after-hours doughnut forays in Weimar; now she was even further removed from her childhood denials and restrictions, those invisible chaperones. They had lost contact, been replaced by a handsome French law student who pursued and persisted, sweeping his new-found love into a world she didn't know existed.

The Welsh student working in the French hotel became

acquainted first with Louis's sisters, Gabrielle, Georgette, and Céline. Their father, Monsieur Gérard-Varet, was also called Louis. Marjorie recognized him as the Rector of the University of Rennes, though she had yet to meet him before her summer at the seaside. After helping with morning housekeeping at Madame Sablé's hotel, she was free until late afternoon tea time so her off-hours were filled with trips to the beach and visits with the Gérard-Varets who stayed in the old windmill *Le Moulin des Ecluses* on the west beach. The *moulin* was probably built before the Revolution to control *des ecluses* or locks that drained seawater through canals into salt ponds. By the early twentieth century there was little left of the once thriving salt business and the windmill tourists eagerly settled into their unique summer *pied à terre* so close to the sea.

A photograph shows Gabrielle and Georgette in a quiet moment reading and doing needlework on a garden bench in front of the restored windmill. More photos show swim parties that included other young students in the area with Louis, his sisters, and Marjorie in the lead. They played tennis, gathered wild flowers and collected butterflies while the law student from Rennes, France and the language student from Wales stole private moments on the islets across the sand bars at low tide.

Madame Sablé became an accomplice. When the Gérard-Varets embarked on excursions to Cap Fréhel or Dinan, they included Marjorie who was fortunate not to be restricted by her working hours at the hotel. When in Dinan, she and Louis were free to explore the medieval alleys of the old fortress town on the Rance River and to discover their own historic sites that Marjorie would return to a decade later. But little did she suspect during that idyllic summer of 1912 the changes that would happen in the meantime. For that moment, that isolated interlude, the only existence was hers and Louis's.

When the sea was calm enough, a fisherman would take the family along with Marjorie out around the headland to Cap Fréhel. Picnic baskets in hand, everyone climbed the bluffs for lunch before finding a swimming spot along the bay for a cool dip. Marjorie and Louis didn't notice the chill of the water. They could swim together forever. Later, everyone huddled close for warmth as the fishing boat headed for home port. Out in the bay the Channel Islands floated on the horizon, glowing orange in the sunset behind the explorers returning to their cosy seaside resort.

Everyone went to a Breton festival, first to the Pardon at the church, then to the music and dancing. Dressed in local costume, Marjorie's by Madame Berthe Guillard, the sisters along with Marjorie posed for the new camera. The music was vaguely familiar, similar to its Welsh counterpart, and Marjorie recognized a few phrases her father had often sung while he was working about Maesyffrwd. When she and Louis and his sisters joined the dances, Louis guided her through the intricate formations, rarely missing a step. It was so romantic to hold on to him, and not let go. She felt she was holding on with her heart. Was this what it meant to be in love?

The season passed all too quickly. By the end of the summer, Marjorie had formed close friendships with Louis's sisters while her attachment to Louis grew more intimate day by day. At last, it was time to leave, and closing the hotel and windmill meant time apart, but everyone had their jobs to do including Marjorie and Louis. They made plans to rendezvous in Rennes as often as possible, and to write to each other daily.

Madame Sablé's list of last minute tasks seemed to grow longer instead of shorter, but finally Eulalie, Marjorie and Madame were in their carriage ready to depart for the train at Dinan. As they rounded the road to the beach, Marjorie caught a glimpse of the Gérard-Varets' carriage by the windmill, still waiting for more boxes and portmanteaus from the three sisters, Louis, their parents and their servants who included a cook. Marjorie stared in disbelief. The boxes were mounted higher than the passengers' heads. Now she understood the source of those beautiful suits the ladies wore on their picnics. She couldn't see Louis. He must have been packing his bowler hat and collars and waistcoats and swim dress. He had a large wardrobe, too.

Surprisingly, the Welsh amateur photographer captured their explorations and excursions, and recorded the lovers' summer of discovery. Tennis rackets, butterfly nets, and bouquets of heather gathered above the seashore were mementoes of treasured times, preserved on film developed in Rennes in 1912, then hidden in boxes in the bottom of Welsh and English cupboards for sixty-five years. When the pictures reappeared, the portraits along with the Breton costumes and the butterfly nets were still sharply defined.

Chapter 8

RENNES II: 1912, 1913

Back in Rennes there was much scurrying to prepare for the returning boarders as well as a new term at the University. Marjorie moved into her old room with the same room-mate from the previous term whom she now tempted with an extra *pain au chocolat* to deliver a letter to the Faculty of Law where Louis studied.

Studying for a diploma in French literature proved to be more demanding than the French language course which had been relatively easy as Marjorie had several years of conversational French from her previous schooling behind her. She now found that reading and translating more complicated verb forms in higher levels of writing required more concentrated study. And concentration was proving difficult with Louis invariably just a few seconds from her thoughts.

Teaching at the University of Rennes in 1912 was Anatole Le Braz (1859 – 1926) who was a renowned Breton scholar and folklorist. He was Marjorie's favourite professor and the person who most encouraged her to study for a Degree Superior in Literature which she completed in the autumn term. Monsieur Le Braz's signature on her parchment diploma was a prized possession; another remnant of her life in France hidden for sixty-five years but still crisply intact when it finally emerged.

Studies continued in spite of liaisons with Louis whenever possible. Perhaps their brisk correspondence was good practice. He wasn't far away – only about two blocks of city streets – but busy with his own law courses when he wasn't writing letters. He sent his messages via the younger brother of his friend at school, and Marjorie received them within an hour of his writing. An hour later he had her reply. It was like an Edwardian mobile telephone with sizzling waves of love being relayed at high speed.

One day early in October both Marjorie and Louis were summoned to the office of his father, the *Recteur*, immediately! Surprised and bewildered when they arrived within seconds of each other, the two correspondents faced each other, mouths ajar, silent. Papa Gérard-Varet broke the silence by reading aloud Marjorie's latest epistle to Louis. Once again she had reiterated her everlasting, unabashed love for his son. In her haste to send her declaration, she had forgotten to write *'fils'* ('son') after 'Louis Gérard-Varet' and the messenger, a friend of the usual go-between who happened to be ill that day, had delivered the missive to Louis Gérard-Varet *pére* (father).

Rector Gérard-Varet was a stately gentleman, solemn in his role as a Director of the University but less severe in his role as father. When he questioned the young students, he was pleased at their sincerity. For the first moments he forgot the differences between Louis and Marjorie. Then he remembered. She was a foreigner, not of their country even though she sounded like a Breton. Would she be a good wife for his only son and heir? Would their love withstand their divergent origins in times of stress and difficulties? Did they even recognize their differences? He had raised his children with more emphasis on intellectual pursuits than ecclesiastical devotions, but what about Marjorie?

He posed these difficult questions to the young lovers and was relieved at their replies. They had given thought to their future, their vision of which was dominated by their wish to remain together. They did not recognize differences, only similarities. Marjorie had not been subjected to a fervent religious upbringing and thought she could conform to the model of a French Catholic wife. She was so sincere that Louis *père* silently wished for this. But he knew she didn't really understand, and he wasn't sure his wife, who knew more about these matters than he did, would be as accepting as he was. He hadn't had time to discuss this delicate matter with her. The passion in Marjorie's letter had demanded quick action.

After another gentle interrogation during which the young couple had again affirmed their love, Louis *père* held their hands in a kind of blessing and declared that although he thought they were too young he would consider them engaged. The wedding, however, would only happen after Louis *fils* completed his law studies. In the meantime, the law school at Nantes would most likely be a less distracting location for his studies.

Marjorie and Louis were thrilled at their unexpected engagement, but not so happy about Louis's transfer to Nantes. And Louis's messenger was sorry to lose those extra centimes of income! Now the letters would be sent by post and take longer, and according to Louis *père's* plan, be less frequent.

Marjorie had to admit that both she and Louis studied more assiduously when they were apart. Louis was just beginning his law studies and had at least three years to complete before they could even think about marriage. Of course they continued to correspond albeit a little more sedately than before, just in case another letter went astray.

They celebrated their engagement in the company of Louis's sisters and parents who held a petite fête in their honour. Marjorie's family was not aware of her new happiness, or her commitment to marry a Frenchman and to live abroad, permanently. No, she wrote to brother Geoffrey in November of 1912, she would not be home for Christmas. 'Weather has been very bad but last few days have been better; it is very cold.' There was no mention of her holiday plans with Louis and the Gérard-Varets.

Nestled under leafy trees in a cliffside park in St. Brieuc no more than one hundred kilometres from Rennes is the statue of Anatole Le Braz together with his friend Margaret Philippe. They are oblivious to the industrial pollution that surrounds them, and ironically not looking into the deep valley of the River Gouëdic that stretches beneath them. Instead they are facing the oasis of the small park and Margaret seems to be telling a story, relaxed and confident in Breton kinship.

In 1912 at the University in Rennes, Monsieur Le Braz became Marjorie's mentor. She needed a confidant, someone to talk to about her new role as the fiancée of the son of the rector of the university, a role M. Le Braz understood. Her new life would be far removed from the experiences of her parents and siblings in Hirwaun. And her new happiness was something they still knew nothing about.

Marjorie decided to tell them when she returned home at the end of term in January. It would be easier to do in person than by letter. She counted on her father's understanding; she didn't expect Jeanie to accept or even condone her daughter's marriage to a French lawyer.

Marjorie explained to Madame Gérard-Varet that she would break the news to her parents when she returned home in January of 1913. She also explained that she would need to stay in Great Britain to work at least for part of Louis's studies over the next three years. Hopefully she could visit during holidays and the time would pass quickly. Explaining to Louis that she would work across the Channel was more difficult, but he finally accepted that she needed a teaching post which she could secure in Great Britain more easily and more lucratively than in France.

Chapter 9

TEACHER IN BRITAIN: 1913, 1914

By February of 1913 the Welsh fiancée of the French law student found herself at Cade House in Heathfield, Sussex. She had been hired to teach young Catherine Gates, daughter of Sir Frank Gates, who had recently returned to England from a government post in India.

Catherine was about eight years old, too young to go to boarding school and also too young to be a companion for Marjorie, who must have felt isolated by her profession as well as her social position. Being engaged to someone in a foreign country where visiting was difficult and sporadic was an obvious hardship, while teaching a few French and German children's songs to a single beginner student offered limited satisfaction for someone who had just completed three years of advanced language study in Europe.

The upheavals of the 'Edwardian crisis' which marked the pre-war years – labour unrest; civil war in Ireland; the women's movement asking for suffrage and contraception rights amongst other freedoms; political instability in Europe – affected everyone in Britain, no matter how covertly they were understood. Marjorie was no exception. She spoke of having some political awareness, but her ingrained reticence resurfaced upon her return to England. What she thought regarding contraception was never spoken about; perhaps it wasn't an issue – yet – between herself and her Catholic fiancé. However, she repeatedly – in her young adult years and through her diaries in later life – referred to her enduring desire to have children. Meanwhile, she dreamed of Louis, and for Christmas sent to Brittany a gift-wrapped portrait-photograph of herself from Merthyr Tydfil in Wales. She didn't speak of delivering this gift in person although it's not impossible to have returned for a visit at least once in the eighteen months she taught in England. Was Louis still an unknown in her homeland? Did she need an excuse to travel again to France?

By June of 1914, about eighteen months from when she started her job, frustration took hold, and Marjorie resigned her post, thinking she could 'not do any more for young Catherine'. There was no real outlet for her skills; she was fluent in German and French and had a musical education. Hopefully another position would prove more challenging and satisfying. She still had more than another year to wait for Louis. Did she have a suspicion, like many other Britons aware of European politics, that war was an imminent possibility?

When she left for her summer holiday back home in Wales, war was declared. It was August 4, 1914. From her notes:

> I gave my notice. Fortunately, because war broke out and almost immediately, Céline, Louis's elder sister, wrote and asked me if I could go out to stay with them and help her nursing at a big hospital in Rennes. The boys' *lycée* had been put to use by the military. Of course I was very pleased to do so. I was to live with the Gérard-Varets for a year. They lived in a palatial apartment above the museum which was just around the corner from the hospital. Louis by now was conscripted to the Flying Corps and was stationed just outside Rennes.

Chapter 10

NURSING AND THE GREAT WAR: 1914-16

THE FIRST TRIP

The first time that I will go to France,
He always said when one spoke to him,
I will bring back huge hats
For my four sisters with violet eyes.
Jane will have the blue, like her eyelids.
Pearl will have the blond, in rice straw.
If the most beautiful eyes are in England,
The largest hats are in Paris.

The first time that I will go to France,
I will picture this wonderful visit,
A boat larger than the pleasure boats
That one sometimes sees on the Thames.
With the blue waves appearing,
I will tell him about our grey ones . . .
The first time that I will go to France,
I wish first to go to Paris.

The heart-rending pleasure of this first trip!
I dream already of the day of departure.
My sisters smiling. My mother less prudent,
Already in her eyes a misty aura.
I will see very soon her hands are shaking
'It is no further than the white birds';
But a little later the hands are smaller;
And the Goodbyes have the air of permanence.

In my new trunk of larch wood,
I will find among other fragrances,

53

— The sweet peas are English flowers —
Four large bouquets of sweet peas.
They will always be there during my happy childhood
Their delicate perfume known so well . . .
An English perfume, when arriving in France
It is a memory without regret.

The first time I come to France,
He said, again, as he died,
It does not resemble my memories,
Little dreams that my heart concocted.
Hit by shrapnel . . . A month in hospital . . .
Then some Latin words without a word in English . . .
The first time that I come to France
It is not as I had believed.

Yes, I am dying. My mother perhaps
Is playing the piano at this moment;
She will weep on reading the letter
That will reach her on the next boat!
My sisters will not have the huge hats,
But they will put flowers on all my photos.
. . . The first time that I go to France
It is still more beautiful than I believed! . . .

Maurice Rostand, translated by Ross Henry

Maurice Rostand was the son of the well-known French poet and dramatist Edmond Rostand, famous for his play *Cyrano de Bergerac* written in 1897. Maurice's best known poem was *The Crystal Coffin*, partly a conscientious objection to the Great War and partly an autobiographical tribute to his strained relations with his father. *The First Trip* (*Le Premier Voyage*) is a lesser known war poem that was printed in a French newspaper, clipped by Marjorie, and taped for posterity inside her nursing Ward Book, its yellowed newsprint legible and clear after eighty-five years.

The First Trip is bittersweet in its imagining of an Englishman coming to the idealized France that is belied by the reality of war. The hats, the pleasure boats, Paris, trunk of larch wood lined with sweet peas – from England. Then the shrapnel and hospital and dying. The war, piano music, flowers on photos. And France still more beautiful than imagined.

Marjorie rushed to France on her second trip, following her dream. After a year and a half, would she find it as beautiful as she remembered? She would work with Céline to help care for wounded soldiers, and be close to Louis who was stationed nearby. The Marne, Somme, Passchendaele, Ypres, the trenches were not yet household expressions. Louis was in the Flying Corps, that new branch of the French military that flew those new biplanes that were eventually equipped for shooting from the air. He cut a dashing figure in his pilot uniform. Marjorie's white overalls and dresses were sewn for her by Louis's mother and were not especially dashing, even if they were flattering to her slim figure. Her photos exude a confidence and an eagerness to nurse. In just a short time the Germans would be stopped, even pushed back to their own borders where they needed to stay. No more Sarejevos; no more Kaisers invading neutral countries for the purpose of war on another country. Margot and Martha and Crystal would still be friends.

The Military Hospital in Rennes occupied the dormitories of the Boys' School around the corner from the Museum of Rennes which in the early 1900s housed the library of the University and where the Gérard-Varets lived on the top floor. Marjorie's room is marked with a box around her window on a photo postcard of *Le Musée* dated January, 1913. Her room is now used as an office and storage space, no evidence of its history recognizable in today's city museum which still exists in the same building.

The Boys' School around the corner is also still a school, but again there is no available history of its being used as a military hospital in World War I. Nevertheless, Marjorie's photos prove the existence of the military hospital at *Le Lycée* where Louis's sister

> Céline, a clever and very serious-minded girl – a little older than myself [Marjorie] – was in charge of a 'service' in a large dormitory in the boarding part of *Le Lycée* and had about forty

55

to fifty beds. The 'service' had a doctor (army) and an intern and about six to eight nurses, all of whom were volunteers – not trained – and three or four what we called stretcher bearers (*brancardiers*). We had no instruments, and to start with improvised dressings. My father sent us out some scissors and forceps. Gradually we became reasonably equipped, fortunately, as we needed them for we received *blessés* (wounded) direct from the front.

Marjorie had no previous nursing experience, let alone war experience. Undoubtedly her naiveté was her biggest ally. She has left no extant diary of her time in the Rennes Military Hospital, but still in existence are her letter of recommendation from the senior doctor after her ten months of service at Rennes; her Ward Book; photos of patients and staff; a few 'souvenirs' from patients; plus her few notes written sixty years later.

Dorothy Cator's memoir *In a French Military Hospital* written in 1915 provides more detail. Dorothy and her sister went together to a French hospital. They were warned 'not to bring anyone too well trained, as conditions under which we worked would be more than they could bear . . . and that we must . . . get on with French military authorities under whom we were working. The necessities were a knowledge of French and tact and readiness to do anything.' Marjorie fulfilled all of these requirements.

Cator goes on to say that most French doctors were supportive – Marjorie's certainly were – whilst some French nursing 'sisters' were untrained and unsuitable and could be jealous of the English girls. She also says there were 'many well-trained and excellent French nurses' and that the French were democratic and less aware of 'bridgeless gulfs between classes in England'. This lack of class awareness must have been one of the great attractions of the French for Marjorie. Here she could be comfortable socially and fit into a work situation that valued her willingness to learn and work hard.

From her notes:

> The Gérard-Varet family were all very good to me – accepted me as a future daughter-in-law. Madame made all my white

overalls and aprons. And so I lived with them for a year and became quite useful to Céline who sometimes had bad days and would trust me – when she could not go to hospital – to do the morning rounds with the Doctors and make the necessary notes and report to her.

Marjorie's Ward Book, along with the poem *The First Time*, is a treasure buried in her box of memorabilia. Scribbled on the inside covers are train schedules for Paris to Le Havre to London along with some patients' signatures and Paris street addresses which may have been later rendezvous points with Louis, when they were both stationed closer to Paris. Ward notes list the patients by name and/or bed number along with abbreviations for diagnosis and/or treatment. Aspirin was a common remedy. One of the patients' names reappears in a photo of a ceremony awarding the French Military Cross, Marjorie looking on along with other hospital personnel. Other photos identify patients and staff, and other notes in her notebook show mini anatomy lessons in French which also help to identify the wounds of the patients, the majority being of *main* (hand) and *pied* (foot). There is also a definition of massage: 'mode of treatment that consists of the application of the movements of hands on the surface of the bodies.' Pharmacy supply notes call for common tea, laudanum, chloroform, lanolin, vaseline, and essence of lavender. Even though some items were familiar, her learning curve was steep.

From her notes:

> Amongst the nursing help we had the surgeon's wife, the Princesse Aymon de Faucigny Lucinge whose husband was garrisoned at Rennes. She was very good to Céline and me. We had also the elderly Duchess de Rohan (dowager, from Brittany) whose family home is the Chateau de Josselin, and with whom the Princess and I (for I was near Paris by then) spent our Christmas Day 1915, the entire de Rohan family being present.
>
> At the end of a year [in fact it was less than a year, approximately ten months], I felt I could not trespass any further on the Gérard-Varet family, so I went home having received the faithful promise from the Princesse de Lucinge that

she would send me word if she heard of a vacancy for a volunteer nurse. True to her word, at the end of the month came a telegram "come at once to me in Paris – bring uniform."

The telegram from Paris to Hirwaun, Aberdare was sent 25 August, 1915. Addressed to Marjorie Thomas, Maesyffrwd, Hirwaun it reads:

> come immediately to me Paris Mrs Tuck holding place for you blue uniforms furnished but bring your rennes white dresses telegraph when I may expect you Lucinge.

Mrs. Tuck and Princess Lucy were both Americans: Mrs. Tuck dedicated to her work with the Stell Tuck Foundation Hospital near Paris that was founded by herself and her husband, and Princess Lucy working with the Red Cross as a nurse and accompanying her French husband who was a doctor serving with the French army. Perhaps their American-English connections helped to influence their decisions to further employ the eager volunteer from Wales. And of course, everyone needed help.

One important item Marjorie obtained before her departure from Rennes was a letter of recommendation:

> Doctor Major Bourdiniere, First Class, Attending Dr. to the Supplementary Hospital No. 1 certifies that Miss Marjorie Thomas worked as a nurse from 15 October, 1914 to 30 July, 1915. She worked very regularly with remarkable competence and with a devotion and zeal above all praise. The Attending Dr. Bourdiniere. Read and approved the Senior Dr. Perrin de la Touche, Rennes, 30 July 1915.

Although Marjorie had no formal training, she was becoming a skilled nurse.

From her notes:

> Off I went, spent the night at the home of the Princess. The following day she took me out to Rueil-Malmaison, a suburb of Paris, to a small hospital which had been built by some wealthy

American for the benefit of the poor of the district, but now taken over by the military. The business end was still run by a *Directrice*; the medical side by the village doctor. [There were] two trained nurses and two volunteers, cook, cleaner, and gardener. I was given board (very good), bedroom and a few francs for pocket money. There we received many severely wounded men direct from the fighting line. A surgeon came out from Paris when operations were necessary. Our first was a young Russian whom we named the "Butcher" as every op-case was fatal. One day when in the theatre I turned to see the patient's intestines billowing out over his body – the surgeon's arm plunged deep inside the abdomen – when he said *'Ponction Gastrique!'* [perforation stomach], and I was sent flying to the Directress for a litre bottle of ether which the surgeon emptied into the patient, and then just sewed him up. We, the nurses were mad – after that the Russian was sacked and a very good Paris surgeon used to come out when necessary.

It was Dr A. B. Lavie, who was particularly fond of Marjorie. In May, 1917 his letter of recommendation states:

I have had in my service from August, 1915 to May, 1916 Miss Thomas, a young English nurse. I cannot but praise her personality and conduct in my service. She has always shown great willingness of spirit, quick action in busy times, tact and complete devotion to duty. In a word she is a young nurse who is very competent and knows her profession very well. Hospital Stell, Tuck Foundation, 19 Boulevard Magenta, Rueil, Seine & Oise, Military Hospital Annex V. R. 6.

A personal note accompanying this letter adds:

Dear Young Lady, No, I have not forgotten a charming young nurse called Miss Thomas. Not only have I not forgotten her, but I often think of her. I am especially happy to send you the certificate you asked me for, which will be sincere and well earned. I am sending you the news that you asked for about our son, happily it is good news. I send you my best wishes and much fondness. Dr. A. B. Lavie 1 May, 1917.

59

This date is a year after Marjorie had left the hospital and returned to Wales.

Obviously, Marjorie had become a well-liked and much-respected *infirmière*. In the first two years of World War I she had not only become a competent nurse, but had also become friends with and visited a princess in Paris; spent Christmas in one of the oldest family *chateaux* in France; and lived for a year with a French family. All of these experiences were exceptional, not only because they were beyond the wildest dreams of a woman from a colliery town in Wales, but because they had killing fields of the Great War as their ultimate credential.

The one constant through this period of intense learning and maturing was Louis, who managed to escape death or mutilation in his highly exposed cockpit. During the First World War 'Flying Aces' became popular heroes, but there was much to be done to warrant such a heroic title. The French, who introduced the 'Ace' system, required a pilot to have shot down over five enemy planes. The Americans likewise to begin with, before they graduated to match the Germans' ten. The British, however, never recognized the system. Louis's name is not on the list of known 'Aces' at London's Imperial War Museum. Instead of flying a fighter, he may have spotted for artillery, taken aerial photographs, or even bombed trenches. Marjorie was relieved when 'occasionally I was able to get off to meet Louis in Paris (he was stationed there at the time); we would meet at the home of a friend of Louis's father.' A restraining chaperon during the passion of war.

One keepsake from this time that surfaced after eighty-five years is a postcard from the Duchess de Rohan to Marjorie dated 8 January, 1916 (following Marjorie's Christmas 1915 at Josselin): 'Many wishes dear young friend for 1916. Your sweet letter touched me greatly. Yours sincerely, Duchess de Rohan.' Posted from Josselin in Morbihan, far from the ravages of trench warfare in the north, and a magnificent setting for Christmas in any century. The sheer walls of the chateau rise from the gentle banks of the Oust River in one of the most spectacular natural castle-settings in France. Originally built before the fourteenth century and with several subsequent rebuildings, this home of the de Rohans claims to be the longest-lived-in family home in

France. A wander through the rooms now open to the public gives a sense of ancient as well as modern life; the relaxed interior and family photos contrast with the ornate centuries-old granite carvings of the façade. The Dowager Duchess that Marjorie knew is probably somewhere in the chateau in a portrait; her presence in Marjorie's war-time photos show her as middle-aged, dressed in nursing apron and overalls and wearing Red Cross credentials, her kindly smile an inspiration to those who worked with her. Marjorie treasured her friendship, as she did that of Princess Lucinge.

In the thunderous traffic and din of central Paris today, just behind the Madeleine, there is a quiet street called the Rue de la Ville l'Evêque (street of the Bishop's town), and behind the street's contemporary row of offices built immediately adjacent to the sidewalk, there is a beautiful neo-classical palace still intact at number 18. It was here that Marjorie spent her first night in Paris in August, 1915, and it is this address that appears on her *Annexe du Passeport*, issued at Southampton on August 27. (Marjorie's preparations for another year abroad didn't take long as she had received Lucinge's telegram only two days before.) It is interesting that her passport states she has no profession, yet the reason for her voyage is to fill the functions of a nurse in a hospital. She never qualified as a professional nurse in spite of spending most of her life nursing in various capacities. It is also interesting that this Passport Annex was all she needed to travel across war-torn France in August 1915, but by the following February, when she went to Wales to see her brother Geoffrey who was home on leave, she had a Prolonged Validation to the Passport Annex issued for fifteen days and officially stamped in London, Southampton and Le Havre. She was also given a Safe Conduct certificate for fifteen days stamped by the mayor of Rueil and allowing her to travel by train through territory in a state of siege to Hospital Tuck Stell at Rueil via Paris from either Le Havre or Boulogne. This must have been in accordance with the rules set up by the Anglo-French Committee in January, 1915 to control 'undesirables' crossing to France. The certificates asked for a statement of loyalty to The Allies (Marjorie's was signed by the Police

Commissioner and the Mayor); a capacity to nurse wounded (she was returning to work at the Hospital Tuck Stell); and a request from a French establishment for permission to travel (the Hospital Tuck Stell). Marjorie became adept at recruiting Military Permits as well as getting herself across the Channel. Her papers indicate that she travelled via Le Havre or Boulogne just as all British army officers and nurses travelled at that time; however, being independently employed she was no doubt blessed with much less red tape at the borders than if she had been with the Red Cross or British military. When she did go home to see Geoffrey, her return was delayed for two days by foul weather; two days that had to be allocated within the time on her certificate.

Rennes was an initiation; Rueil was confirmation. At Rennes she learned the rudiments of nursing in a crude setting; at Rueil there was a real civil hospital providing more sophisticated care for more serious military wounds. An anonymous nurse in *Diary of a Nursing Sister at the Western Front 1914-1915* describes 'bad cases . . . awful mouth, jaw, head, leg, and spine cases who can't recover, or will only be crippled wrecks. You can't realize that it has all been done on purpose, and that none of them is an accident or surgical disease.' Ambulances direct from the front arrived at Hôpital Stell in a steady stream, at one point averaging eighty patients a day, and Marjorie became skilled at the staple dressing of tincture of iodine after swabbing with lysol. Sometimes she had to 'close her ears to the cries of pain' from which she could only briefly escape.

At Rueil-Malmaison she was in the familiar setting of electric trams commuting to an elegant city; however, the image of war with zeppelin raids and nightly spotlights over Paris cast an alarming shadow. She was still close to Louis, but their rendezvous times were sporadic and brief. Controlling their desires must have placed a strain on their relationship, and perhaps was a critical factor in Marjorie breaking her engagement just a few months after leaving Rueil. The waiting, holding everything in check, seemed interminable.

Rueil-Malmaison overlooks Paris from hills that rise above a loop in the River Seine. Elegant mini palaces dot the large woods that have existed for centuries and provided park-like settings for the wealthy bourgeois who settled there around the turn of the last century. Edward Tuck and his wife Julia Stell, successful American entrepreneurs who preferred France to the United States, built their Château de Vermont near Rueil in 1900 and in 1903 the Hospital Tuck Stell, offering free medical care to the indigents of Rueil. Rueil was a fairly wealthy suburb of Paris and the hospital a model for modern health care. In 1930 the Stell-Tuck Foundation concluded its charitable work, another floor was added, and today the building functions as the basis for a large medical centre for the area. The colourful *Mairie* where Marjorie had her travel documents stamped is now graced by a large First World War memorial erected in 1920, a tribute to those victims from Rueil that comprised a small fraction of the holocaust, some of whom would have been known intimately by Marjorie.

Down the street from the *Mairie* is the church, its soaring steeple rising to a God that Marjorie was forced to recognize which seems at odds with Dorothy Cator's report that the role of the French Catholic church was difficult to ascertain as the French military authorities did not encourage priests in the hospitals. Céline was probably the most religious of all the French Marjorie encountered, and even if the *curé* was not encouraged in the wards, Marjorie had her own rosary in case a patient needed it. It was the war that brought Marjorie face to face with Catholicism. The same war that forced her to accept the familiarity of injury and death. A war that put Louis's life in constant danger, and that made Paris a cruel crucible for two would-be lovers. All took their toll.

When Ieuan begged once again for his daughter to return to Hirwaun to help him, as all his assistants along with his medically-trained son were fighting in the war, Marjorie left France 'very reluctantly'. Had it been less beautiful than she had hoped? Visibly, hospital war-nursing was vastly different from her previous university and seaside-resort escapades; emotionally, romance was threatened by war and peril; psychologically, the gulf of differences was deepening.

Marjorie kept several souvenirs of the War, but she did not

reveal them until the last decade of her ninety-seven years. She never said there were painful memories, just secret ones. They evoked another life, one she experienced in her youth and which had little relevance to her later life. She became adept at separating different periods of her life, not allowing consequences from one episode to affect another. Or so she believed.

Tucked away in her box at the bottom of a cupboard is a Zouave coloured drawing with a camel motif dated 1914 and signed 'Ozary 2039'. There are two photos of Baizid Ben Ali in his full Zouave regalia of fez, embroidered bolero-jacket, cummerbund sash, baggy pants and puttees. In one photo he is next to another exotically dressed soldier wearing a turban, head and neck scarf, cape and baggy pants. He is standing next to a man in a French military jacket and riding breeches. Together they form an international trio for war. The formal portrait-photograph of Princess Lucinge signed 'Souvenir de la Guerre 1914-1915' is perhaps the most poignant of all.

On a postcard piece of art paper, A. de Saint Jean asks Miss M. Thomas of Lycée no 1 at Rennes if she 'will permit me to offer you a souvenir'. On the reverse side he has drawn with pen and ink a farm scene of hay-gathering with a windmill in the background. The drawing is signed 'A. de Saint Jean 1915'.

These pieces offer evocative historical connections to this extraordinary period, but for Marjorie there are other, more personal connections. Her favourite brother Geoffrey is 'leading a charmed life' in the Artillery in the trenches; her younger brother Ben is on mine-sweeper duty with the Royal Navy; her youngest brother Glyn is in the Army Service Corps; and Louis is still in the French Flying Corps.

On a broader scale the invincibility of the great British Empire and its ability to protect the weaker nations of the world has become a dubious boast, whilst 'Keep the Home Fires Burning', the new patriotic song by Welshman Ivor Novello, hums on everyone's lips.

The Russian Revolution in 1917 will soon have far-reaching effects. The idea of workers uniting against profit-hounding mine owners has spread seeds of discontent, and the teachings of communism have already begun to take hold, even in Wales.

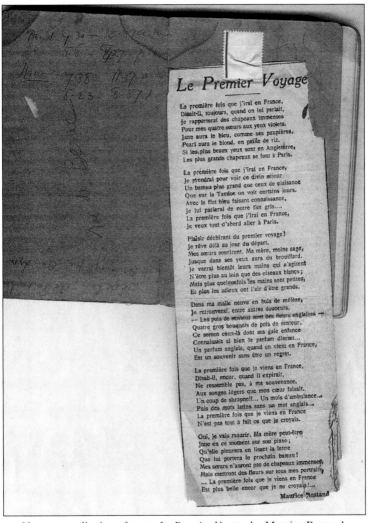

Newspaper clipping of poem *Le Premier Voyage* by Maurice Rostand.

French pilot Louis Gérard-Varet
poised for take-off in WW1 biplane.

Georgette Gérard-Varet, sister of
Louis, souvenir photo for Marjorie.

Louis and sisters Gabrielle, Céline and Georgette reading military
correspondence.

Renaissance façade of Chateau of family de Rohan at Josselin, Morbihan, France where Marjorie spent Christmas, 1915.

Chateau Chardonneux on the river Sarthe, WW1 home of Princess Lucinge.

Captain Geoffrey Lynn Thomas,
Military Cross, killed in action
6th June 1918.

Geoffrey's grave, Marfaux British
Cemetery, Marne, France.

Geoffrey Thomas, 95th Brigade, Royal Field Artillery, 1914.

Marjorie at the Mumbles, South Wales coast, 1920.

Maesyffrwd, 'the doctor's home', Hirwaun, Glamorgan, Wales.

Dorothy Thomas on Alderney, Channel Islands, circa 1917.

Ieuan and Jeanie Thomas with grandson William Henry, 1933.

Portrait photo of Marjorie taken for Louis, circa 1913.

Chapter 11

DISPENSING AND NURSING, ENGLAND AND WALES: 1916 TO 1926

After three years of education abroad and two years working as an untrained volunteer nurse in the Great War, Marjorie returned to the land of her childhood and to Maesyffrwd, the imposing Edwardian home that was known in the town until its collapse from neglect in 1991 as 'the Doctor's'. She was twenty-five years old. Soon after his daughter's arrival, Ieuan moved to a new surgery, but at the old surgery Marjorie found:

> Father's surgery overflowing with surplus drugs, drawers full of instruments – all persuaded to have been acquired by the drug travellers – also piles of bills for the same, plus many accounts from motor firms.
>
> Right, I said, nothing more from the drug firms until all the accounts are settled [she was able to send more instruments and supplies to Céline], and I had the help of the kindly accountant to the colliery to unravel the intricacies of the motor car accounts which were grossly overcharged.

Ieuan was one of the first owners of a motor car in South Wales. His obituary (newspaper clipping, Radyr, November 1936) called him a 'pioneer motorist', and his escapades as a 'sportsman of repute' were legendary. 'As an officer in the Volunteer Corps, Dr Thomas was a noted marksman and a regular member of the South Wales team that competed annually at Bisley. On one occasion about 20 years ago he won a trophy at one of the Bisley competitions.' So it must have been from her father that Marjorie inherited her adventurous nature!

With the move to the new surgery there was room for living quarters for a gardener-chauffeur, and with the arrival of Hatch, who lived and worked with the family for many years to attend to the BSA motor car, Marjorie's automotive duties ceased. But initially she did have to 'unravel the accounts'. Later, even through the early Depression years of her marriage, her husband always had a car, but she never learned how to drive. Perhaps her father's muddled accounts were a determent.

In the new surgery which was a converted old inn there was enough room for a 'large consulting room, big waiting room, dressing room, toilet, dispensary, and living quarters for a gardener-chauffeur and his family.'

When Marjorie first arrived in June, 1916 she was immediately 'sent to the Dispensary of Queen's Hospital in Birmingham to learn something about dishing up medicines – pills and powders.' This must have been a brief course as within weeks she was entrenched in Hirwaun sorting pharmaceutical bills as well as the motor car accounts.

Once back in Hirwaun:

> As well as being dispenser, and doing all the surgery dressings, I also became what you might call the District Nurse for Father's patients, there being no official District Nurses in those days, only midwives.

District Nurses did not arrive in Hirwaun until the 1930s, and then they were paid by collections gathered by volunteers. Fifteen years earlier Marjorie was paid £2 a week by her father, serving also as his dispenser, who according to Nansi Selwood in *A History of the Villages of Hirwaun and Rhigos* also 'held classes in Home Nursing in which he not only introduced new ideas but also gave sound practical advice.'

From Marjorie's notes:

> I loved working for my father, but did not like living at home, so I arranged to take a secretarial course in Dispensing offered me by the pharmacist at Queen's Hospital in Birmingham. I studied hard and Father let me off for six weeks to go back to Queens for some practical before the exam. So I took and passed the Apothecaries Hall Exam, and felt myself equipped to apply for an outside post. I was soon established as dispenser in

a very nice practice near Bristol – but not for long, for I yielded to Father's begging me to go back to help him. He would give me £2 a week instead of £1!!

It seems there was no escape. But if she really wanted to, there was nothing to stop her from returning to France – and Louis – especially if she was willing, at least temporarily, to relocate as far as Bristol to get away from home. However, hovering over everything was the reality of her situation with Louis. She continued to face that interminable stretch of time: first the war which was beginning to seem endless and was now being called the 'Seven Year' or 'Ten Year War'; then the completion of law school. How long would she have to wait to realize her sexuality, to become a mother, to be loved? What if Louis were seriously wounded or maimed? She had seen so many men torn to pieces, then fearful of returning to girlfriends or wives incomplete, ripped apart, wounded emotionally as well as physically. And most important, perhaps the most significant factor she had to consider, was the isolation and disconnection from her family she most surely faced if she married a French man and went to live in France.

More from her notes:

> I was quite happy at work – even doing an evening surgery once in a while – using a bit of common sense and some "rep:mists" [repeat prescriptions] to see me through. This would happen when Father had gone shooting into the country, ending up in a kind patient's pub, 'Mrs. Jones, the Lamb' who would ply him too freely with whisky. He would forget surgery; but woe betide him when he got home, for Mother's tongue was sharp. Father was not a drinker, but would have these bouts of over-indulging, only very occasionally. He developed bad stomach trouble, and was eventually operated on in London by the famous Mayo Robson [co-founder of the renowned Mayo Clinic in America. It wouldn't however be until 1924 that Ieuan suffered his first stroke.]

Marjorie was a natural nurse. Her learning was hands-on and her war experience invaluable when it came to handling dressings and miners' injuries. She never went down into the pits though. Indeed this would probably have been impossible for her because of her claustrophobia. But her father occasionally had to descend to the scene of a severe accident.

Tumultuous seems an inadequate description for the happenings of 1916 to 1918, but their violent commotions and confused emotions were soon to embroil Marjorie.

Whilst still in France in February of 1916, Marjorie travelled through war territory and across the Channel to see Geoffrey, which was fortuitous as it was their last time together. After ten days in Hirwaun, she returned to Rueil and Louis, but her father's requests for her to help him instead of the French were never very distant. Finally in July she yielded as she was aware that she had gained valuable experience and that her father was over-worked and unable to get help.

The Conscription Act of January 1916 had made armed services compulsory for all single men aged 18 to 41. One could apply for an exemption if employed in a 'necessary job' such as farming and coal mining. However, many miners would view the army a better alternative to 'going down', and gladly enlist. The statistic of 350,000 British casualties in the three months preceding October 31, 1916 had not yet become reality. 'The Somme' was only just becoming a synonym for death.

Other historical highlights of 1916 would include the uprisings in Ireland, especially the Easter calamity in Dublin; 50,000 cases of syphilis reported amongst service men; David Lloyd George from Wales would become Prime Minister of Britain. Dr Marie Stopes remained tireless in her campaign for women's sexual education, as did the suffragettes' campaigns for the women's vote: women over thirty would be enfranchised in February 1918, and Dr Stopes would eventually publish her revolutionary *Married Love* in July 1918. Nothing moved with ease for these champions of women's rights in spite of the independent status of women workers in the munition factories along with the ambulance drivers, tram conductresses, police, and even the WAAC (Women's Army Auxiliary Corps) combining to produce unprecedented social, sexual and political changes for women in Britain.

Marjorie's freedom in France had been unprecedented for her

time although she wasn't the only young British woman to work independently in France during the war. Nevertheless, she astounded her conservative parents who by wartime knew of her relationship with Louis. Their biggest fear, of course, was illegitmate pregnancy. Marjorie didn't speak of close supervision or chaperones; who were these Parisian friends of Louis's father's at whose houses she and Louis met whenever they could? Perhaps her parents' – more harshly her mother's – primary concern was losing their valuable daughter to a foreigner in a foreign land. If Marjorie stayed in France or returned immediately after she had come home, would she ever come home again? Who would help Ieuan in the practice and Jeanie in their home?

Marjorie was caught – Louis in France; Father in Wales. She wrote:

> During my time at home, after the work of morning surgery, dressings coped with and the tidying up done, I would go home where if there was any special cooking to be done – cakes, sauces, etc. – I would undertake to do it. Incidentally, although there were two maids in the house, I was expected to get the breakfast. Afternoons were spent studying for my exam or dressmaking. Life was very dull. Louis and I corresponded regularly, but I began to think very seriously about our attachment. It was going to be some time before he would be released from the Flying Corps: then would come three or four years of study before there would be any chance of marriage. I could have had other menfriends, but was too conscientious to allow the friendship to develop. So after much thought I asked Louis if meanwhile we could consider ourselves unattached. Reluctantly he agreed and correspondence ceased.
>
> But two years later he wrote and begged our relationship to take up again. Very serious thinking ended in my saying 'No'.

In some ways it is difficult to understand this decision of Marjorie's, whilst in some ways it seems obvious given the lovers' conflicting circumstances. It was toward the end of 1916 and she had been engaged for four years. Passion heightened by war was suppressed by the war. However, Louis would not have expected this from a fiancée who would normally be more rather than less willing to give him support during such a dangerous time. He must have been very perplexed by her decision, and obviously did not take it lightly. She spoke of other male friends, yet compulsory conscription along with the death toll of the 'lost generation' of the Great War compromised their availability. But Marjorie was getting older, and if there were other chances, they were slipping through her fingers. She was fulfilling her filial duty; the omnipresent war remained a big interference.

Sometime in 1917, Dolly had married the soldier son of the Vicar of Alderney, Channel Islands, a marriage her parents 'would have nothing to do with'. The reason for this estrangement is unexplained, but Marjorie knew that her mother would never travel to France and might even prevent her father from doing so in the future. This fact, along with Louis's being French, ensured that her parents would no more have anything to do with her marriage than with Dolly's. But Dolly did not have to move to France.

Regardless of her parents' antagonism, Marjorie enjoyed a holiday with the Vicar's family on Alderney when Dorothy became engaged. The wedding took place at the home in south London where Dolly worked as a governess, and with whose family she had holidayed on Alderney when she met her future husband. Dorothy did not return to Hirwaun until the birth of her son, Henry on January 28, 1918, but Marjorie missed the new arrival at their family home, Maesyffrwd, because of the Apothecaries' Examinations in Birmingham on the same date. It was after this that Marjorie worked in Bristol for a brief period. Louis seemed to exist in the past. But the war continued.

Dolly remained at Maesyffrwd for several months after the birth of her baby, then later in the year went to Germany with her husband after Armistice was declared on November 11, 1918. She stayed in Germany for a year, leaving Henry to the care of Marjorie and Auntie Maud, Ieuan's sister who had lived at Maesyffrwd for several years following the death of her brother Edgar. Marjorie wrote:

> Auntie Maud and I looked after Henry. We made little suits for him out of our old skirts, etc. He slept in my room, and many

nights for hours I paced the room, nursing him because he had earache. This trouble later in his teens became serious. An operation caused the loss of a facial muscle, but this did not cause much damage to his looks.

Whether she chose to be or not, Marjorie was a surrogate parent to her sister's child for this first year from November 1918 to November 1919 and again when Henry spent another year at Maesyffrwd when he was six years old and his parents were in Edinburgh, where his father studied mine management. Henry remembers Marjorie teaching him French proverbs or sayings, especially *'Qui se ressemble s'assemble'* ('Birds of a feather flock together') and *'Parmi les aveugles le borgne est roi'* ('Amongst the blind people the one-eyed man is king'). He also remembers seeing stowed in the glass-fronted bookcases in the study the two volumes that Marjorie had won as music prizes at Howell's School, which Marjorie had forgotten were there. It is not surprising that she forgot as there was no piano in her home, and no evidence of musical entertainment. All the new dispenser and acting district nurse (and surrogate parent) in Hirwaun could do was dream of operas and Celtic dancing in far-away Europe. They seemed as remote as having children of her own. When Louis wrote again at the end of the war asking to resume their relationship, it must have been a heart-wrenching 'No'. In her diary (begun in 1981 when she was 90) she wrote:

> At one time, I thought, when I gave up Louis, 'I shall never have any children' and one evening when staying in Etretat [on the north coast of France in 1924] with my father, I walked up the hill to the fisherman's chapel and prayed that one day I would have children.

One can't help wondering if she had her rosary with her.

Years later Henry followed in the Thomas family footsteps and became a surgeon, practising in and around London. It was his cousin Ben, Ieuan's fourth child who took over Ieuan's practice in Hirwaun in the early 1930s.

Ben knew the territory. He had his early schooling at Penderyn and then Aberdare, before going on to Epsom College and then St. Mary's Hospital in London. When he returned to Hirwaun he inherited a legacy of sympathy and understanding left by Ieuan who knew his miners well. Ieuan understood when someone needed a day off, and even though they couldn't present any immediate symptoms worse than the usual black-lung cough or backstrain, a sick note could excuse them from a shift and medication in hand would prove something was not right. The 'sick' patient would appear at the surgery, and through to Marjorie's dispensing room would come a prescription note for 'A.D.T.', their code for 'any damn thing', and 'the patient departed with a bottle of Rose Water or some Infusion of Gentian'.

The miner was happy with his day off and any damn thing, but Marjorie often had to face another damnably dull day at home. Though she liked her work well enough, she felt tied to her family. And apart from a few short months studying dispensing and working in Bristol, she was tied to them from autumn of 1916 until the summer of 1926. From her 25th until almost her 35th birthday.

Chapter 12

KILLED IN ACTION: JUNE 1918

THE VISION

For him, no more the clarion call to arm,
The horror of the conflict, bursting shell,
All the dread sounds and sights of war,
Are over. Now, for him—all's well.
But, when the slowly rising moon
Floods all the fields with silver, he will pass,
White, with the sweetness of the rest from pain,
Pale, in proud sorrow, noiseless o'er the grass!

Mary A. Wylie

Geoffrey was killed June 6, 1918, one day after his twenty-fourth birthday. 'He was in command of his battery, and in the act of communicating by telephone important information to a brother officer who was in charge of another battery when he was struck by a splinter of shell and fatally wounded.' Mary Wylie's poem is preserved on a yellowed slip of newsprint along with Geoffrey's death notice. There was much proud sorrow at the Thomas home at the news of his death.

Marjorie wrote:

> He seemed to live a charmed life. For four years all the injury he received was a kick on the leg playing football. He became a very good-looking man and a well-loved companion to his fellow officers.

These comments are reiterated in the letters from his fellow officers and friends written to his parents. 'The news caused a genuine grief in all the Divisional Artillery. He was one of the most popular officers we had . . . He was always so unfailingly good-tempered and cheerful and kind ... On Friday we buried him at the Military Cemetery W.N.W. .... The General came and several other officers and a number of men from his battery.' Another lieutenant tells 'that a shell burst and wounded him slightly while a splinter killed your son who was 50 yards away. Mercifully death was instantaneous.'

His Commanding Officer explains how 'I had given him command of the battery and was going to apply for him to be given it permanently as Major.' ... nor a better friend could possibly be found. One sees quite a lot of death here but I have never had one touch me as much as that of your son. At the time of his death he was just going to speak to me on the telephone ... The enemy were making an attack when it happened, and the battery was being shelled. He had been bucking up the men at the guns, taking no notice of the shells – and had just walked across to have breakfast when the shell came ... The Brigade is still fighting hard, or what is left of them, but I wanted to take the first chance I had to write to you. Your son was well known and popular with the whole Divisional Artillery and I expect you will have many letters of sympathy from the many friends of "Tommy" as he was called by everyone. I am indeed filled with sorrow at his loss.' Geoff 'Tommy' was not coming back; he would not write any more letters with 'absolutely no news'.

Marjorie was devastated by her beloved brother's death and turned to Princess Lucinge for solace. The Princess wrote from her Château de Chardonneux in Ecommoy, Sarth (south of Le Mans and about halfway between Rennes and Paris):

Dear little Friend,

Your pathetic card told me the sad, sad story of your great loss and how my heart aches for you!

I know that you loved him and how proud you were of him and now you have only those brave memories to console you. How I wish I could send you some word that could really comfort you but there are none and only time, kindly time will take away the sting and let you feel that there was never a nobler ending to a young life.

74

May God give you strength to bear this affliction – and your poor Father and Mother! Will you tell them how much I sympathize with them in this great sacrifice.

I came down here 10 days ahead of my permission for a reason which I can't write you & soon I go to the Chatel Guya to take a cure for I am very tired and used up. My husband is well and has been recalled from the front & put with the Americans which is a great relief to me. I am just told that I can say that there is an American base here and our châteaux are filled with officers and soldiers so I came to try to arrange to make them as comfortable as possible under all conditions.

Our hospital at Paris had been reduced by evacuations until there were only 8 blessés instead of 60 – out here our ambulance is full 65 beds and I have just come back from my work there.

Again, dear little Marjorie, I send you my heart full of loving sympathy in your terrible bereavement and remain

Aff'y yours

Prin Aymon de Faucigny Lucinge

Château Chardonneux on the River Sarthe is just north of the more famous French Renaissance châteaux of the Loire region and is not unlike Chenonceaux with its steep-roofed towers covered in slate tiles. Rounded turrets and a classical façade of ochre and white stone with wrought-iron balcony railings add to its grandeur. Since the First World War it has seen many occupants; currently it has lost its interior elegance and houses a facility for repatriating French foreign nationals, an international setting not unlike its role almost a century ago. Just when Princess Lucinge lived in her lovely château for the last time is not known, but in 1918 it must have been a welcome retreat from war-torn northern France even though it had been converted into officers' quarters and a hospital. She writes with the news that Hôpital Stell has been evacuated. Marjorie is now far away from those realities of injury and strife, but her few saved letters from Geoffrey epitomize the struggles of the Great War:

22.10.15 B.E. Force France

Dear Marjorie,

Thanks very much for your two letters also the cigarettes. Please don't send any more for a time because Father sent a huge lot the other day. Mother also sent me cake and chocolates. I expect you are very busy now with all these wounded coming in. Are you leaving the place at Xmas? I should certainly do so if I were you. I suppose you know by now that we were pushed up into the Battle of Loos for our baptism of fire. We got into action on the Sunday morning (26th Sept). We had a devil of a time. I never expected to come out alive. The Huns spotted my battery and let us have shell after shell. Fortunately they were excited and their shelling was erratic. Still they were quite near enough and some much too near. They shelled us with the 4.2 inch guns. A nasty shell to hit one in the 'pot'. Loos is one mass of ruin now even most of the cellars under the houses have been shelled in. The Huns left lots of ammunition in these cellars & in cellars under the church so they shelled these places in order to try and explode this ammunition. They failed to do so. The whole of the battlefield was strewn with dead, and our gun position was practically amongst them. It was really horrible. We had an observing station down in Loos & to get there we had to walk down the Germans' old communication trench which was floored with dead. We found lots of things in these trenches. German letters and cigars, cigarettes. Some of the trenches had holes in the side which led into huge rooms nearly as big as a house with beds in and beautiful furniture. In these places Germans were found alive with telephones three or four days after they had been driven out. I must now dry up.

Hoping you are well.

Heaps of love
Geoff

Another newspaper clipping reads: 'Lt. Geoffrey Lynn Thomas, R.A. – An ammunition dump being set on fire, he led a party and extinguished the flames, displaying great courage and coolness. He set a fine example to his men.' For this action Geoffrey was awarded the Military Cross.

Trenches floored with dead; large underground rooms with beautiful furniture; ammunition dumps burning; heroism in the face of death – even though Marjorie had heard these stories before, her brother made them be a part of her. A letter before they met on Geoffrey's last leave shows the manoeuverings involved to meet each other on home turf just for a few days:

29.1.16 B.E. Force France

Dear Marjorie,

Got your letters the other day. Well at last my leave is settled. I am leaving France on the 6th February (Sunday). Don't know what time I shall arrive in England. You had better get to England on the 5th or morning of the 6th. You can find out what time my train gets to Victoria on Sunday. If by any chance we miss one another I will be at Ben's digs. I think I will spend the night (if I arrive in the evening) at the Regents Palace Hotel near Pic. Circus. You had better book two rooms, one for me and one for yourself unless you arrange to go somewhere else. I expect we shall find one another alright. Will leave London the next day. I have a fair amount of shopping to do on the Monday. Don't forget the 6th Feb.

Love
Geoff

This letter lists all the priorities: a hot bath at a good hotel (rather than at brother Ben's digs); time for shopping (the men on leave always had long lists of things needed to replenish their kit); and connections to go home.

Another letter, undated, typifies trench warfare:

Dear Marj,

Thanks very much for all your letters & PCs. received lately. I had nothing much to do this morning so thought I had better drop you a line. I hope you had a good time in H'west [Haverfordwest]. How did you find the two old Dames? I suppose the town is just the same as it was when we used to go there? The weather today is awful. It is raining in torrents and things are very miserable. It is not so bad here when fine but when it rains it is absolutely awful. Yesterday was a perfect day.

77

To cap it all this afternoon my C.O. wants to see me so I have to ride four miles through mud and rain up to the guns. Am not looking forward to it. I have written quite a lot of letters this morning. I have absolutely no news.

Heaps of love to all

Yours
Geoff

This may have been Geoff's last letter to Marjorie. Most of these letters went through the censoring stations and were copied by a censor who not uncommonly forgot or was not allowed to date them. But Marjorie was in Wales visiting their old stamping grounds, and Geoffrey was obviously a bit nostalgic in what was possibly his last letter home.

Chapter 13

MARRIAGE: AUGUST 1926

The far-reaching effects of the Great War are almost impossible to comprehend. Marjorie has lost both her French fiancé and her beloved brother. She is working in a job she never imagined just a few years before. She has completely lost touch with her life in Europe except for occasional correspondences and over the years some vacations in France, sometimes with girlfriends and sometimes just with her father.

There are postcards from St. Malo, Mont-St-Michel, and Dinard in 1924 and 1925, all reminiscent of Marjorie's first time in France. Perhaps significantly, there is not one from St-Jacut. Most of the cards are addressed to Mrs. I. G. Thomas, saying that she should come too. But of course she never does. On one note Marjorie asks if the new car has arrived. There is also a card from Ieuan from Madeira in 1924 that demonstrates that his eyesight is failing, perhaps due to cataracts. He has also had a slight stroke.

In 1924 she takes her father for a visit to Paris and to Geoffrey's grave at Marfaux near Rheims; then on to the Normandy coast at Etretat where Ieuan writes in a post card to his wife that Marjorie has not found company there other than himself. He is unaware of her expedition to the fishermen's chapel where she will pray that she might yet have children.

Sometime in 1925 (there is no date) Marjorie again writes to her 'dear mother' from Dinan in Brittany. She thanks her for her letter and asks how Dr Henry is as her mother 'hasn't mentioned him once'. She also asks for the train times from Paddington to Cardiff, and says she has just had a 'wonderful lunch of lobster, potatoes, cheese, cherries, cider and lovely bread and butter. The Mediterranean fleet is in so the town is very gay.' Once again, this is a big change from Hirwaun. However, other changes are beginning to take shape at home. Marjorie has enquired about Dr Henry, the new assistant for her father, and her mother refuses to answer.

In December 1924, Dr Bill Henry, like Ieuan in 1888, graduated from medical school at Edinburgh University, and Hirwaun is his first appointment. He is Scots, a year older than Marjorie, and prefers to remain silent about his experience in the trenches at Ypres. Following his war experience, his quiet determination pushed him through medical school where he could just pay his costs. At last, in Ieuan's practice he is able to claim a salary and have a few coins in his pocket. He is well liked, a 'very kind and gentle man'.

Dr. Bill and Marjorie work well together in the practice, as well as in their personal lives. He stays for a year (1925-26) and their relationship flourishes, so well that her parents

saw how the wind was blowing and decided that Bill should be asked to leave – reason: I had become too useful to the practice. I begged Bill to get in first, so he said he would like a change and soon found a post in Whitehaven, Cumbria which he hoped would lead to a partnership.

Whitehaven is a nice little town, but vision of a partnership soon vanished for Bill was told by a friendly practitioner in the town that this doctor's assistantships never ended in becoming partnerships.

I went up to see Bill and we decided to get married, having heard through my sister's husband who was a mine manager [in Yorkshire] that there was a possible vacancy for a medical man in a newly developed coalfield on the Yorkshire moors.

So on August 23, 1926 we were married at a remote country church in Breconshire [St. Mary's Parish Church at Ystradfellte]. The elderly vicar was a patient of my father's. We had two days honeymoon in Cheltenham, then made our way up to Yorkshire where Bill was fortunate, being offered the vacancy already mentioned, and receiving the pleasant approval and good wishes of the two practitioners in the neighbouring little town.

How Marjorie's parents could have considered the ultimate sacrifice of their eldest daughter for their own well-being by ousting Bill, minus Marjorie, is an alarming question. These expectations were extreme, especially as their son Ben qualified as a Bachelor of Medicine and of Surgery in 1919 before going on to several years of surgical training in preparation for assuming Ieuan's practice in the late 1920s. But however one wants to interpret her parents' selfishness, it was Marjorie's own latent feistiness and sense of self-preservation that prevailed and extricated her from her parents' clutches once and for all. Louis and the medieval alleyways of France she has recently revisited are in the past; Dr Bill Henry and a colliery town in England are her future. She will be thirty-five years old in two months.

The wedding is an informal affair in Ystradfellte. The vicar is William Jones; witnesses are Ieuan and Sarah Jane Thomas, John Watt (probably a friend of Bill's), and Elsie Courtenay Cole, Bill's sister. Marjorie's residence at the time of marriage is given as Heolrhydings which was most likely a local farm of one of Ieuan's patients in the parish of Ystrafellte and conveniently borrowed for the required local address as one had to 'live' in the parish for three weeks in order to be married in the parish.

The honemoon is short. Marjorie's arrival in Moorends, Yorkshire, becomes yet another beginning in a strange land, but this time with a beloved partner at her side. There are still years of hard work ahead, moments of heartbreak and happiness, but her tenacity is formidable. She clings to life, to her family, to her husband, and eventually to her memories with a fortitude unimagined until she reveals *Any Damn Thing*.

EPILOGUE

Marjorie and Bill lived and practised for almost thirty years in Moorends, a mining town at the end of the Yorkshire Moors. They had three children: twin boy and girl born on their first wedding anniversary, and another boy in 1933. The early years were lean ones in the lead-up to the Depression that would be followed by another world war. Marjorie's stoicism learned early in life never failed. She needed it in Moorends.

When she first arrived, the pit had just been sunk. There was no electricity, no pavements; and only one shop, which did not even sell the paraffin for their lamps,

> so on Saturdays we would walk two miles to the nearest small town [Thorne] to fetch a tin of paraffin, a little meat, a loaf of bread, and a six-pence packet of Robin cigarettes.

Did she allow herself the memories of electric trams, Paris boulevards, *the Kaufhof*? She probably didn't have time for such luxuries. Her beginnings as a wife and mother were a million miles removed from such sophistication and comfort. As she herself admitted:

> We were established in a little colliery house with the blessing of the Pit officials because we did not voice our political opinion. The doctor already practising to most of the miners was very 'red'. So were the men. Too much so for the Pit officials who set to work to rearrange the terms of the Sick Fund, money for which was deducted from the men's wages. The men were to choose the doctor they wanted, that is to say for themselves and attendance on their wives and families. The men themselves were insured, and their payment for medical attendance came per the state.
>
> Times were hard, but we were young and happy [Marjorie

82

was 36 on October 27, 1926, Bill was 38 on August 2]. So we sat and waited for patients. They came slowly, for the 'reds' were belligerent. Our first patient was a pregnant woman who wanted a tooth extracted – consternation!!! But we did have a tooth forceps pinched from my father's surgery. The operation [was] successfully performed and the woman became one of our most loyal patients and friends.

We received no income until May 1927. It was seventeen pounds. Off we went by bus to Doncaster to enjoy a steak dinner. We each had about two hundred pounds in the bank and lived and furnished on this, orange boxes or the like being for a short time our tables and containers. We were given a ton of coal by the Pit and paid them about fourteen shillings a week for our little house.

By the time the twins were born we had settled down nicely, the number of patients growing steadily and our financial position becoming more stable. At the end of five years we had built a nice house (on ground purchased from the Pit Company) with a very good surgery at the street end of the garden.

This house still stands on West Road in Moorends, the surgery converted to a garage. The house where the twins were born is at the end of a terrace on High Hazel Road. Their auspicious arrival was marked by surprise:

Two babies were unexpected, for the first having been delivered, the doctor went to wash his hands, with the nurse running after him: 'Come back Doctor, there's another to come!' Strange he had not noticed – he was an experienced baby doctor.

Consternation! Marjorie surprised everyone again! After some initial frightening problems with the newborn boy (who spent his first few weeks in a dresser drawer as there was only one cot), the twins thrived and six years later welcomed a baby brother. Marjorie was forty-two by then and one wonders if she still considered herself 'young'.

One of the great sorrows of her life was the death of her youngest son from Hodgkin's disease when he was only eighteen. His ashes were sprinkled over the River Skirfare under a great plane tree near the bridge at Arncliffe in the Yorkshire Dales, his favourite fishing hole. On the very bottom of Marjorie's box of mementoes rests an unframed 9 x 14 watercolour of the spot by artist unknown. Was this something she looked at only in private?

Frugality marked the early years of her marriage, and became a habit difficult to overcome. By the time she died at 97, however, she regretted that she had little money to leave to her children. But the survivors – the twins – were comfortably situated. Her son was an Edinburgh graduate in medicine like his father and grandfather and a practising anaesthetist in Canada where he emigrated soon after the Second World War, and where he still lives. Her daughter a trained physiotherapist married and living in England. A monetary legacy was not therefore needed. What both children really wanted was more stories of her life before they were born, stories they didn't hear until after their father died as it wasn't proper to speak about old boyfriends in front of one's husband. But it wasn't just Louis. There were many other adventures to unfold and explore, snatches of which Marjorie gradually revealed and which in turn have formed the basis of this book.

Marjorie's Bill was much loved and respected by everyone who knew him. Marjorie speaks of him as 'a good gentle man – all that could be desired – and a good husband'. Nevertheless, they had some difficult times. Later in his life Bill suffered several bouts of depression which, he later confessed, stemmed from a mutual attraction he had shared with another woman. Marjorie never entirely believed this; she thought that Bill was unduly guilty over a minor flirtation that had escaped her notice. But after Bill's death, perhaps this revelation made it easier for her to remember Louis. At one point she even said that if she had her life to live over again, she would have married Louis. But would she have? Could she have?

Louis's descendants are still alive in France. Sadly, his son, who was Marjorie's son's contemporary, died whilst this book was being researched. Family members have graciously given permission to reproduce the photographs of their ancestors, but more history of the family remains unknown.

Dr Ben is a Hirwaun legend. Many people still remember him and praise his 'old-fashioned' kind of doctoring. He never turned anyone away who needed help. One woman who lived near his home remembers the gypsy women who would regularly wait at his gate for Dr Ben, who could be relied upon for a meal or for dressing of their wounds following a domestic altercation. And his advice given after a few whiskies was the same as the next day when sober. Ben retired to live in Penarth about ten years before his death in 1968.

Marjorie's death on November 5, 1988 marked the end of an era, and almost the end of a century. Her ninety-seven years outlasted all of her brothers and sisters, and it is she that has left the most descendants of Ieuan and Jeanie's line of the Thomas family – one son living, four grandchildren, five great-grandchildren, two nieces and one nephew. This story is dedicated to her daughter Jean who spent many hours of her days over many years of her life caring for Marjorie in her infirm years. Jean died suddenly of a cerebral haemorrhage in 1999, eleven years after her mother and before all the pieces of this story came together. But it remains their true legacy.

page 12
Llewellin's butter churns; *Haverfordwest*, The Archive Photograph series, Chalford Publishing, 1997.

page 13
Benjamin Thomas, poet, lecturer, author; *Dictionary of Welsh Biography*, 1940.

page 14
class hierarchy; *Class in Britain*, David Cannadine, Yale University Press, 1998.
The Matter of Wales: Epic Views of a Small Country, Jan Morris, Penguin Books, London, 1984, 1998.
Welsh Anglican Church; *A History of the Villages of Hirwaun and Rhigos*, Nansi Selwood, Penderyn, 1997.

page 16
Miss Kendall was in charge; *Howell's School, Llandaff 1860 – 1960,* a brief history.

page 18
höhere Mädchenschulen; *My German Year,* I.A.R. Wylie, Mills & Boon Ltd, London, 1910. *German Education Past and Present*, Friedrich Paulsen, Ph.D. trans by T. Lorenz, Ph.D., T. Fisher Unwin, London, 1908. *Education in a Prussian Town*, Herbert Macartney, Beatty, blackie & Son, London, 1907.

page 19
book of travel coupons; Thomas Cook's *Continental Time Tables, Tourists Handbook, and Steamship Tables,* August 1909.
Edwardian costume; *The Edwardians*, Paul Thompson, Paladin, St Albans, Herts, 1977.

page 20
'Colloquial German'; Thomas Cook ibid p. XXXVIII.

page 24
Nibelungenlied and Wagner's Operas; *Kobbé's Opera Book*, ed. The Earl of Harewood, G. P. Putnam's Sons, New York, 1987, pp. 214-263.

page 27
'We enjoy what is old . . .'; *Weimar Past and Present*, Rainer Wagner and Roland Dressler, Thiele & Schwarz, Kassel, Germany, 1995, p. 54.

page 29
Undine; *Kobbé's Opera Book*, ibid.

page 30
Weimar; *Weimar Past and Present* ibid.

page 31
Marlene Dietrich; *Marlene Dietrich*, John Kobal, Studio vista, London, 1968.

page 32
Pfaffenwinkel; *Germany the Rough Guide*, Gordon McLachan, Penguin Books, London, 1999, p. 99.

page 33
Welfenmünster; ibid.
royal property was forcibly sold; Chronik des Steingadener Rüstzeitenheims, Max Zwissler, tr. Ross Henry, Steingaden, January 1999.

page 40
current fashion; Blackwoods' Edinburgh Ladies Magazine & Gazette, vol 38, p. 143. *The Edwardians*, ibid.
Rennes; *Michelin Tourist Guide to Brittany*, Watford, Herts, 1995. Rennes Plan Touristique, Office de Tourisme, Rennes, 2000.

page 42
St Jacut; *Michelin Tourist Guide to Brittany* ibid. *Brittany and Normandy*, Mary Elsy, B.T. Batsford Ltd, London, 1974.

page 47
Anatole Le Braz; *Brittany and Normandy,* ibid p. 51.

page 56
Dorothy Cator; *In a French Military Hospital*, Dorothy Cator, Longmans, Green & Co, London, 1915.

page 58
Stell Tuck Foundation; Bulletin de la Société Historique de Rueil-Malmaison, Mairie de Rueil-Malmaison, No. 8 October 1983.

page 60
WWI 'Flying Aces'; *The Courage of the Early Morning,* W. Arthur Bishop, Heinemann, London 1966, p 62.

page 62
Anglo-French Committee; Imperial War Museum Reading Room, microfiche France 1.1.
Diary of a Nursing Sister; *Diary of a Nursing Sister on the Western Front 1914- 1915*, anon, Blackwood & sons, London 1915.

page 64
Keep the Home Fires Burning; *Hirwaun and Rhigos* ibid p. 149.

page 66

District nurses; *Hirwaun and Rhigos* ibid p. 156.

page 68

350,000 British casualties; Chronicle of Britain, J. L. International Publishing, Chronicle Communications, Farnborough England 1992.

women workers; *Women at War 1914-1918*, Arthur Marwick, Fontana Paperbacks, Trustees of Imperial War Museum 1977. *The Deluge. British Society & the First World War,* Arthur Marwick, Macmillan, London 1965.

page 75

struggles of the Great War; *The Deluge* ibid. *True World War I Stories*, Sixty Personal Narratives of the War, Robinson, London 1997 & 99. *Goodbye to All That*, Robert Graves, Jonathan Cape/Penguin, London 1929. *Memoirs of an Infantry Officer*, Siegfried Sassoon, Faber & Faber, London 1930. *Testament of Youth 1900-1925,* Vera Brittain, Chatto & Windus, London 1930.